A CONCISE HISTORY OF

FLORIDA

JAMES C. CLARK

THE
History
PRESS

Published by The History Press
Charleston, SC 29403
www.historypress.net

Copyright © 2014 by James C. Clark
All rights reserved

Cover photos courtesy of Florida Archives Photographic Collection.

First published 2014
Second printing 2014

Manufactured in the United States

ISBN 978.1.62619.618.6

Library of Congress CIP data applied for.

Notice: The information in this book is true and complete to the best of our knowledge. It is offered without guarantee on the part of the author or The History Press. The author and The History Press disclaim all liability in connection with the use of this book.

All rights reserved. No part of this book may be reproduced or transmitted in any form whatsoever without prior written permission from the publisher except in the case of brief quotations embodied in critical articles and reviews.

*To a new generation of Floridians, Elizabeth Mattei,
R.J. Clark and Taylor Clark.*

CONTENTS

ACKNOWLEDGEMENTS

This book carries the name of a single author, but it is really the work of dozens of people whose research and encouragement proved invaluable in writing it. At the University of Florida, I was fortunate to study with legendary Florida historians David Colburn, Samuel Proctor, George Pozzetta and Michael Gannon. They produced two generations of Florida historians. Many of those I was fortunate enough to study with have become leaders in the study of Florida history, and their work contributed to this book. Jane Landers at Vanderbilt, Sherry Jackson at Florida International University, Andrew Frank of Florida State University, Susan Parker of the St. Augustine Historical Society, David Tegeder at Santa Fe College and Steven Noll at the University of Florida all produced work that made my journey much easier. The University of Central Florida has become a major center for the study of Florida history, and I am grateful for the work of Connie Lester, Dan Murphree and Robert Cassanello, who have done much to advance the study of the state's history. Dr. Jerrell Shofner, the former chair of the UCF History Department has been a source of inspiration for nearly three decades, and his work in Florida history has always helped me.

Jon Findell of the University of Central Florida's Faculty Media Center continues his role of friend and great source of help. Ray Arsenault and Gary Mormino of the University of South Florida, Paul George of Miami-Dade College, Jack Davis of the University of Florida, Mike Denham of Florida Southern College and Tracy Revels of Wofford College did significant work to aid this book. The work of journalists Joy Dickinson of the *Orlando Sentinel* and Craig Pittman of the *Tampa Bay Times* have helped in my research.

Adam Watson of the Florida State Archives has again come through with the help I needed, as has Cynthia Cardona Melendez of the Orange County Regional History Center. At The History Press, Alyssa Pierce and Julia Turner have shown great patience in working with me, and I am thankful. I am especially grateful to Laureen Crowley whose editing made this book what it is.

1

SETTLING FLORIDA

More than ten thousand years ago, as the great glaciers began to melt, Florida began to take shape. It had the same general shape as it has today, only it was twice as wide. St. Petersburg would have been one hundred miles inland during this period. As the glaciers melted, the sea level rose, and the peninsula of Florida was reduced to its present size. (The Florida peninsula is so distinctive that astronaut Neil Armstrong said Florida was the first shape on earth he recognized as he returned from his walk on the moon.)

Four thousand miles away, ice created a bridge from Siberia to Alaska, allowing people to enter North America. They scattered across the continent and reached Florida nearly sixteen thousand years ago.

The first Floridians hunted animals far different from those found today. They hunted bison, camels, mastodons and mammoths, but when hunting wiped those creatures out, the people turned to more traditional game such as rabbits and deer. Florida's first settlements formed around springs, such as Warm Mineral Springs in present-day Sarasota.

The people who settled along the coastline moved farther inland as the sea level rose. By 5,000 BC, the Florida climate had become what it is today.

The population increased, and the native tribes built villages. Archaeologists have found that around 2,000 BC, the tribes made fired-clay pottery.

By 500 BC, there were established tribes throughout the peninsula, including the Timucuan, Calusa and Apalachee, with smaller tribes in more far-flung locations. The Ais lived near the Indian River, Creeks and

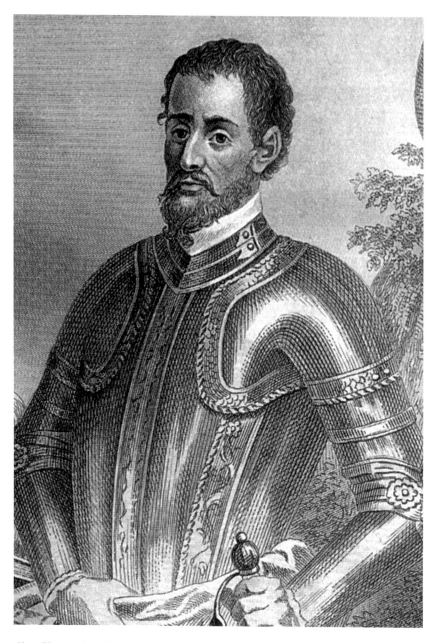

Above: Hernando de Soto led an expedition through Florida and what is now the southeastern United States. *Florida Archives Photographic Collection.*

Opposite: Credited with the European discovery of Florida, Ponce de León named it after the "Feast of Flowers." *Florida Archives Photographic Collection.*

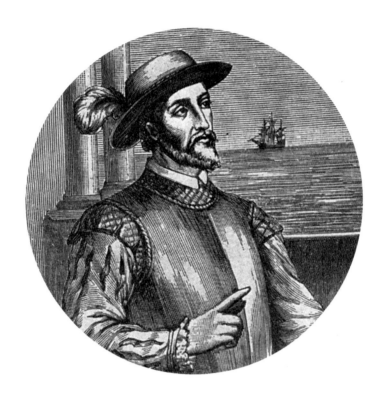

Choctaws in the panhandle, the Matacumbes in the Florida Keys and the Tequestas in southeast Florida.

The Timucuans established a number of villages in north-central Florida. They grew corn and gathered fruits and berries. The Timucuan villages featured a cluster of small huts surrounded by a circular twelve-foot-high wall of tree trunks. They had a rigid feudal system with a chief and council.

The Calusa Indians in the southern half of the peninsula lived in nearly fifty villages.

The population estimates vary widely; however, by the time the Europeans arrived, there were between 100,000 and 300,000 people in Florida.

There was one tribe that would become synonymous with Florida that was not present—the Seminoles. They were late arrivals, not moving into Florida until the 1700s.

Although Juan Ponce de León gets the credit for the "discovery" of Florida, there are indications that the peoples of the Caribbean islands, such as Cuba, moved between the islands and Florida much earlier. The people who came might have been looking for slaves and avoided publicizing their voyages. Crude forms of Florida first appear on maps around 1500.

TIMELINE 14,000 BC-AD 700

14,000 BC: The first people arrive in Florida.

9,000 BC: Glaciers melt, and Florida shrinks. The peninsula was once twice as wide.

7,500 BC: People hunted, gathered and started settlements during the Archaic period.

5,000 BC: First semipermanent settlements in Florida.

4,000 BC: Settlements are established along the St. Johns River and near present-day Tampa.

3,000 BC: The late Archaic period sees settlements on the coasts and along riverbanks.

2,000 BC: First fired-clay pottery comes into use.

500 BC: Mound building takes place along the Crystal River.

AD 700: Indian tribes, including the Timucuan, Apalachee, Calusa and Tequesta, are formed.

One sign that the Spanish had come before is seen in the hostile reaction Ponce de León and other explorers received. The Indians had apparently encountered the outsiders before, and the experience was negative.

The Columbus expedition in 1492 set off waves of Spanish exploration that stretched from Hispaniola to Peru. Florida was a late addition to the Spanish Empire.

The knowledge that there was gold in the New World led to a gold rush by the Spanish. The search for wealth drew people of various backgrounds. Thousands of poor Spaniards enlisted in the military for a chance to claim a share of the wealth. The Spanish practiced a system called primogeniture, which meant that the eldest son inherited the vast majority of the father's wealth, leaving younger sons to fend for themselves and causing many of them to seek fame and fortune in the New World. After Spain's wars with the Moors ended, soldiers sought new adventures.

The adventurers, known as conquistadors, came to conquer the Indians and make their fortune.

Conquistador Ponce de León originally came with the second voyage of Christopher Columbus and was later named governor of Puerto Rico. The son of Christopher Columbus challenged Ponce de León's position as

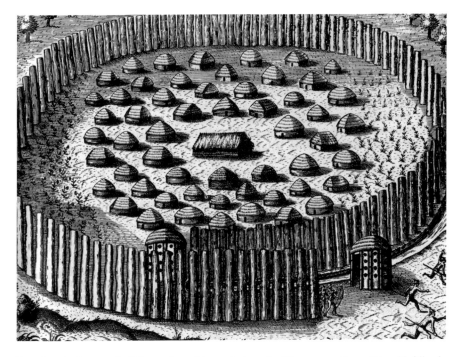

French artist Jacques Le Moyne drew this rendering of a Timucuan village. The chief lived in the larger structure in the middle of the compound. *Florida Archives Photographic Collection.*

governor, and as a consolation, the king of Spain granted Ponce de León a charter to go look for new lands. On March 3, 1513, his three ships sailed north, and on April 2, they sighted land. He named the cape he rounded "Cape Canaveral," the first European name for a point in North America.

He named the territory *La Florida*, or "feast of flowers," because it was the Easter season, and he claimed it for the king of Spain.

No one is sure where he landed, the original North American mystery. It was probably near present-day Melbourne, although there are many claims and no proof.

Wherever he landed, the reception was probably not what he expected. The natives attacked and injured three of his crewmen. Ponce de León fought back just enough to get his men to safety. The attack was unprovoked; perhaps the natives had encountered other Europeans who sought to enslave them. When he reached his second landing site at Jupiter Inlet, Ponce de León was attacked again. Then, while sailing around the keys and up the west coast, he was attacked twice more.

For three weeks, he wandered along the coast and then returned to Puerto Rico. It was seven years before he returned. He planned to come back sooner; however, his wife died, and he needed to care for his daughters.

When he did come back, it was to establish a settlement. He brought two hundred settlers—men and women—along with farming implements, plants and animals. Where he landed is unknown, but it was on the southwest coast near Port Charlotte.

The natives there were no friendlier than the ones he had encountered on his voyage seven years earlier. As the Spanish left the ships, the attacks began. There were three attacks, and Ponce de León himself was shot with an arrow in his thigh.

He ordered a withdrawal to Cuba, where he died of infection—perhaps from a poisonous arrow.

There was another expedition in 1528, this one led by Pánfilo de Narváez, whose luck was no better than Ponce de León's. Narváez was a classic conquistador, seeking plunder but finding only misery and death waiting for his three hundred men. Only a handful of the members of the expedition survived.

Hernando de Soto came in 1539 with a royal contract that gave him the power to explore and govern Florida and spread the Catholic faith. He came with 537 men and landed on the west coast of the peninsula.

After landing, he found Juan Ortiz, a survivor of the Narváez expedition who had been living with the natives. They walked and rode their horses for three long years, wandering through what is now the southeastern United States, although their exact route is uncertain. The Spanish claim ran to what is now Washington, D.C., and west to the Mississippi—if they could hold it.

The De Soto expedition spread European diseases throughout the region, wiping out large numbers of natives. Among the dead was De Soto, who died of disease on the banks of the Mississippi and was buried in the river. His men—their number reduced by two hundred—made their way to Mexico.

Luis Cancer arrived in 1549, sent by the viceroy of Mexico with three other missionaries to Tampa Bay. As he went ashore, he was clubbed to death by the natives. The survivors returned to Mexico.

Tristán de Luna arrived a decade later, sent from Mexico with 1,500 settlers and soldiers to the Gulf Coast. He proved to be a terrible leader, and the expedition failed.

The Spanish were ready to give up on La Florida as not worth the money and lives. On September 23, 1561, King Philip II announced that Spain no longer had an interest in settling Florida.

Between 1513 and 1560, not a single Spanish settlement was built.

2

THE FRENCH CHALLENGE

King Philip II's decision to abandon Florida might have stood if not for the French. Like children who express interest in a toy only when another child wants to play with it, Florida recaptured the Spanish imagination only when France wanted it.

In France, the Protestants—known as Huguenots—sought religious freedom from the government, which often persecuted them. The Huguenots fled to nations throughout Europe and to North America.

In 1562, Jean Ribault was selected to lead an expedition to North America, accompanied by his aide, René de Laudonnière. He landed near Cape Canaveral and then sailed north to the mouth of the river the Spanish called the St. Johns, which Ribault renamed River of May, after the month he arrived.

He and the Timucuan Indians became friends, regularly exchanging gifts and food. When Ribault returned to Europe, he made a brief detour along the way to establish a colony in present-day South Carolina.

The British jailed Ribault briefly, and Laudonnière took over the French mission. For centuries, it was thought that the French built Fort Caroline at present-day Jacksonville, but no trace of the fort has ever been found. Recent research suggests that the three-sided fort was located in present-day Georgia, not Florida. The colony had several hundred residents but not enough soldiers. Laudonnière was a weak leader, and his colony was plagued with problems. After being released from jail, Ribault returned to try to salvage the French settlement.

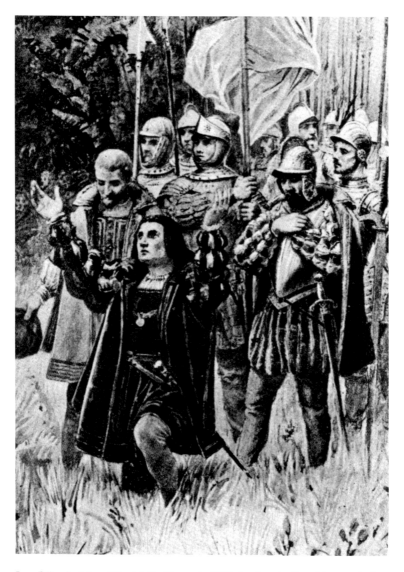

Jean Ribault claimed Florida for France in 1562, leading the Spanish to settle the territory they had originally decided to ignore. *Florida Archives Photographic Collection.*

The Spanish were alarmed by the French presence, which was along the Gulf Stream, the route for Spanish ships laden with gold. The Catholic Church also was concerned that the French Protestants would convert the Indians to the Protestant faith.

THE ST. JOHNS RIVER

For centuries, the St. Johns River was the lifeblood of Florida, bringing tourists and industry to the state.

The Indians called it the "River of Lakes," and the Spaniards initially called it "River of Currents." Sailing along the east coast of Florida, the Spanish saw streams empty into the Atlantic and named each of them. They had no idea where they led, and overeager mapmakers often filled in the details, showing nonexistent waterways that reached the Gulf of Mexico.

The river is unusual because its waters flow north. The first Spaniard to see the river was Juan Bono Quexo in 1520. However, it was the French who first tried to settle the area. In 1564, the French erected Fort Carolina where the river reaches the Atlantic Ocean. Jean Ribault renamed it the River of May, but the French settlement lasted only a year, and the Spanish renamed it River of St. Matthew.

The mission of St. John was along the river, and gradually the river took the name of the mission, Saint Johns. As late as the mid-1700s, both St. Johns and St. Matthew appeared on maps. There was confusion about the spelling of St. John. Some maps read, "St. Juan's," "S. Jean," "St. Wan's" or "St. John's." During the British period of control from 1763 to 1783, the name St. John's was universally accepted. When Florida became a U.S. possession, the apostrophe was dropped, and it became the St. Johns. The river stretches 310 miles from its headwaters in Indian River County to the Atlantic.

King Philip II dispatched Pedro Menéndez de Áviles to remove the French settlement. Menéndez sailed with three hundred soldiers and settlers whose occupations ranged from wealthy noblemen to criminals. The group also included female colonists.

In August 1565, the Menéndez fleet reached the mouth of the St. Johns only to find Ribault's five ships blocking the entrance. Menéndez sailed south to a protected harbor and set up camp at St. Augustine, about thirty miles south of the French settlement.

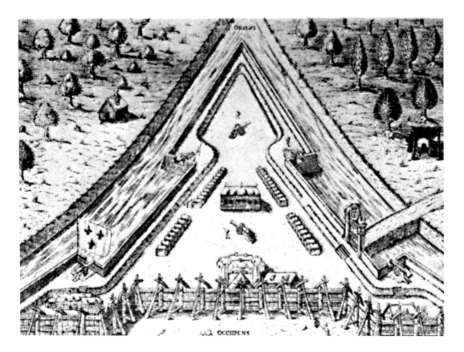

The French built Fort Caroline in 1564 on the banks of the St. Johns River. The move brought the Spanish back to Florida with a landing in St. Augustine a year later. *Florida Archives Photographic Collection.*

Ribault decided it was time for a dramatic move and set sail to attack the Spanish as they unloaded supplies. A storm came up that pushed his ships past the Spanish fleet and wrecked them on the shore south of St. Augustine.

Menéndez launched two attacks, north overland to the French fort and south to the wrecked French ships. Fort Caroline was built to prevent an attack from the sea, not the land side, and the Spanish captured it easily, killing 142 of the French soldiers before the remainder surrendered. The French ships crashed south of an inlet, and the soldiers could not cross the water. Trapped, they were easy targets for the Spanish.

In groups of ten, the Frenchmen had their hands tied behind them and were executed. The spot became known as Matanzas Inlet—or Massacre Inlet. Only a handful survived—those who were Catholics and young cabin boys.

With the French threat removed, the Spanish controlled the colony for the next two hundred years.

3

SPANISH RULE

Florida was assigned to the Spanish governmental unit called New Spain, which included Mexico, Venezuela, the Caribbean islands and Central America.

Pedro Menéndez de Áviles and the Spanish were firmly in control, and Menéndez set out to undo the damage previous conquistadors had done in cruel dealings with the Indians. He signed a treaty with the Calusa tribe and began trading with the Indians, although problems with the Timucuans continued. The Timucuans attacked San Mateo and destroyed the fort.

To defend Spain's territory from foreign threat, Menéndez built four forts from St. Augustine to South Carolina. Soldiers were also stationed at Cape Canaveral and Biscayne Bay to guard the Spanish treasure ships sailing along the Florida coast.

Spain found vast wealth in the New World. There was gold and silver by the boatload and islands that produced fortunes in sugar and rice. Florida was the poor relation, a land without any mineral wealth, poor crops and a financial drain on the rest of the empire. Menéndez was a good governor, but it was not a good assignment for any Spaniard interested in wealth or glory. Being named governor of Florida was the bottom rung on the Spanish Empire ladder.

Florida was the only Spanish colony to never show a profit. The wealthy colonies supported Florida, money given grudgingly and usually late. The payment, known as the *situado*, came once a year and was brought by what became known as the *situado* ship. The *situado* ship provided hard currency

THE SPANISH FORTRESS

In all, the Spanish rebuilt their fort in St. Augustine nine times before building a structure made from sea shells that they named Castillo de San Marcos.

The Spanish controlled the fort for nearly a century and then turned it over to the British, who renamed it Fort St. Mark. The Spanish reacquired Florida in 1783, and the name went back to Castillo de San Marcos. When the United States acquired Florida in 1821, the fort was renamed Fort Marion, in honor of the Revolutionary War hero Francis Marion. The fort fell into disrepair, and the moat became a dumping ground for garbage. Cattle grazed on the grounds.

Control of the fort changed hands again during the Civil War, when Rebel soldiers occupied it for nearly a year. They abandoned the fort to fight elsewhere, and Union troops took control. After the war, it was used as a warehouse and then a prison for Indians captured in the West. Finally, in 1924, it was declared a national monument, and its original Spanish name was restored.

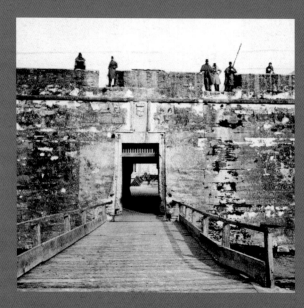

Union soldiers patrol the walls at Fort Marion in St. Augustine in 1863. The Spanish named it Castillo de San Marcos, but the United States changed the name to Fort Marion in 1821. In 1942, Congress changed the name back to San Marcos. The Union captured the Confederate fort in 1862. *Florida Archives Photographic Collection.*

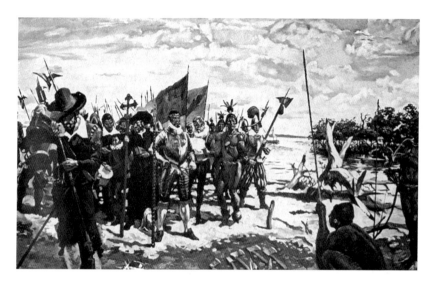

Pedro Menéndez de Áviles established the first successful Spanish settlement in Florida in 1565. *Florida Archives Photographic Collection.*

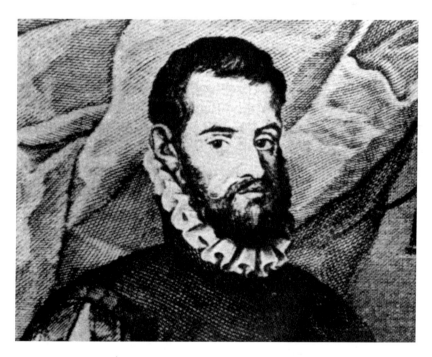

Pedro Menéndez de Áviles settled Florida in 1565 in response to the French settlement. *Florida Archives Photographic Collection.*

THE FOUNTAIN OF YOUTH

Millions of schoolchildren were taught that Spanish explorer Juan Ponce de León came to Florida in search of the fountain of youth. It seems not to matter that Ponce de León came looking for the same thing as every other Spanish explorer—wealth, empire and slaves.

The legend of the fountain of youth dates back nearly one thousand years; some place it in Asia, others in various parts of Europe. Somehow, the myth stuck to Ponce de León.

During Ponce de León's lifetime, no one ever mentioned him in connection with the fountain, and it was not until the 1800s that there was widespread speculation about the location of the fountain. Some said it was Silver Springs near Ocala or Green Cove Springs near Jacksonville. Perhaps it was the St. Johns River itself. In 1934, a promoter generated tremendous publicity by announcing that the fountain was at Bal Harbour. In 1945, a headline in the *Sarasota Herald-Tribune* reported "Fountain of Youth Is Discovered Near Here." Most of the stories came from real estate promoters trying to sell land.

In 1870, a St. Augustine real estate promoter named John Whitney bought some land with a small spring, which he named

for the church and government employees—nearly all of the nearly five thousand residents—and also food and drink.

The Spanish crown wanted Menéndez to stay along the shore to protect its treasure-laden ships, an area where it was difficult to grow crops. Farther inland, it was possible to grow crops, but they competed with crops being grown in other areas of the Spanish empire and were discouraged.

The Catholic Church put constant pressure on the king of Spain to maintain Florida to support its missions—the goal was to convert the Indians to Catholicism. The Jesuits came first, establishing missions as far away as Charlotte Harbor, St. Lucie Inlet and Tampa Bay. The job proved to be more than the Jesuits could handle, and they were replaced by the Franciscans, who extended the missions into present-day Georgia and Tallahassee. Shortly after its formation, the mission system came under pressure from colonial powers.

"Ponce de Leon Spring" and began calling it the fountain of youth. He sold visitors water and tried to sell them land.

In 1904, Luella Day McConnell arrived in St. Augustine from Alaska. She had purchased land with money she had made in the gold strike in the Klondike Gold Rush of 1898. In 1908, she sailed for Spain, telling everyone she was looking for proof that her property was the site of the fountain of youth.

When she returned, she "discovered" a giant cross of stone that she said was hidden by a large tree. She also said she found a box with a salt holder that she claimed was given to Ponce de León by Christopher Columbus. There was also a piece of parchment she said detailed Ponce de León's landing in St. Augustine.

In truth, McConnell planted the evidence. But it worked, and soon tourists flocked to her property to drink the water and buy souvenirs.

McConnell died in an automobile accident in 1923, and her property passed to her manager, Walter Fraser, who turned McConnell's creation into one of the state's leading tourist attractions. He tirelessly championed the legitimacy of his attraction, even threatening to sue those who publically doubted its authenticity.

In 1586, the English privateer Sir Francis Drake attacked St. Augustine and destroyed most of the small city. Spain responded by building the massive Fort San Marcos, a fortress made with a mixture of seashells known as *coquina*. While the fort itself withstood attacks, the neighboring buildings remained targets.

While the Spanish remained concerned about the French expansion, it was England that represented the greatest threat. Gradually, the French and English ate into Spanish claims. In 1588, the British defeated the Spanish Armada, a battle that shocked the world. It marked the beginning of the long, steady decline of the Spanish Empire, which continued over the next three centuries.

The biggest threat to Spain's holdings in North America came from a group of British settlers who landed at Jamestown in 1607. The group settled on land the Spanish considered part of their empire. The Spanish might have been able to wipe out the Jamestown colony if they had acted quickly. Instead, the Spanish abandoned plans to attack. The Jamestown residents nearly starved to death their first year. But when they survived, the British colonies spread south, and the Spanish empire shrank.

The English settled in South Carolina in 1658, and Florida became more of a target. There were raids on St. Augustine in 1665 and 1668. Gradually, the Spanish mission system began to crumble. Queen Anne's War in the early 1700s brought renewed attacks on the Spanish Empire in North America. The war involved Indians, France, England and Spain. In 1702, South Carolina governor James Moore led 1,200 militia members in an attack on St. Augustine. The stone fort held, although Moore destroyed the village and nearby missions.

The impact of the English advances can be seen in the plight of the mission system. In 1655, Spain had seventy friars and claimed twenty-six thousand converted Indians. Half a century later, there were just twenty friars and four hundred converted Indians.

In 1733, Great Britain established the colony of Georgia, which put more pressure on Spanish Florida. Georgia governor James Oglethorpe organized his militia to attack St. Augustine in 1740 and lay siege to the fort in 1742. Spain sent a fleet from Havana to repulse the attack. At the Battle of Bloody Marsh, the Spanish were turned back. It was the last Spanish attempt to hold back the English.

4

THE BRITISH PERIOD

The French and Indian War brought an end to Spanish rule in Florida. From 1754 to 1763, the French and their Indian allies battled the English for control of North America. Spain allied itself with France, and when the French lost, Spain paid a significant price.

During the war, the British captured the crown jewel of Spain's New World empire: Havana. The Spanish desperately wanted it back and offered Puerto Rico and Florida in exchange for Cuba. The British took Florida, giving them the entire East Coast of North America. Spain kept Puerto Rico, and as a consolation prize, Spain received all the land of the Louisiana Territory west of the Mississippi River, plus New Orleans.

On July 20, 1763, Britain took control of St. Augustine and the following month moved into Pensacola. By February 1764, only eight of the several thousand Spanish colonists remained. They abandoned hundreds of homes, and most never received any compensation.

Of particular concern to the Spanish was Fort Mose, a colony founded for escaped slaves in 1738, whose population numbered several hundred by 1763. Many Fort Mose residents left for Cuba with the Spanish while some joined Indian tribes.

The British occupied Florida for twenty years; however, their impact might have been more significant than that of the Spanish in their occupation, which lasted nearly two hundred years. The British took control rapidly, breaking Florida into two colonies with capitals in Pensacola and St. Augustine to make their large acquisition more manageable. The dividing

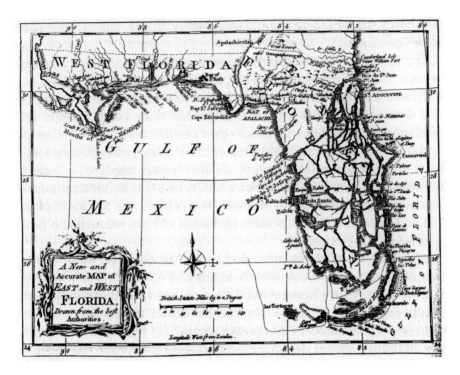

This 1765 map envisioned a network of rivers and lakes that crisscrossed Florida. The map appeared in a London magazine two years after the British acquired Florida. The magazine said East and West Florida was "likely to become a very beneficial acquisition to this nation." *Florida Archives Photographic Collection.*

line was the Apalachicola River. Like the Spanish, the British learned that Florida was a financial drain and operated it as cheaply as possible.

The British had two advantages over the Spanish: they could lure settlers from the northern colonies and could offer trading opportunities. While the Spanish had outlawed trade with the British colonies, now it was encouraged. Trade flourished as rice, indigo and lumber were shipped to Charleston, Savannah and other ports.

The British government also saw in Florida a chance to solve its problems with the Indians. Perhaps settlers could be lured away from the Indian lands west of the Allegheny Mountains to Florida. England began advertising land to those willing to settle, and former British soldiers could receive special grants. The London Board of Trade offered 20,000-acre tracts with each prospective resident receiving 100 acres. Britain gave away 2,856,000 acres in East Florida and 380,000 in West Florida.

PROTECTING THE MANATEE

Concern for the manatee goes back hundreds of years. As early as the 1760s, the British government discussed the threats to the manatee.

The Lords of His Majesty's Right Honorable Privy Council for Plantation Affairs gave the new governor of East Florida instructions about his new job. In addition to dealing with the Indians, defense of the territory and finances, protecting the manatee was included as a requirement of his governorship.

Under "Additional Instruction" to the governor, there was concern that "several Parts of the coast…near the point called the Cape of Florida are frequented and resorted to by the animals called Manatee, or the Sea Cow." As with the U.S. government today, the British king was concerned about protecting the manatees from fast-moving ships or from pirates.

The British interest in the manatee was primarily economic. The British Crown was intrigued with the "quality of oil they produce" and thought "great profit" could be "made by persons carrying on this species of fishing." The new governor was ordered not to sell land near places "frequented by these animals, where they have their Colonies or landing places."

The manatees faced a greater threat from the nearby Indians, who used the creature as a source of food.

Britain allowed its form of slavery, a great lure for southern plantation owners seeking fresh land to replace the land worn out by cotton crops.

The Church of England replaced Spain's Catholicism as the official religion. The British, under the leadership of East Florida governor James Grant, made peace with most of the Indians under the Treaty of Fort Picolata, which established firm boundaries.

Grant encouraged cotton and rice crops, and he built his own plantation near St. Augustine.

A settlement at New Smyrna turned into a disaster. Grant's friend Andrew Turnbull brought nearly one thousand Greeks, Italians and Minorcans to a sixty-thousand-acre settlement. Turnbull dreamed of a Mediterranean colony, but from the start, things went terribly. There was not enough food for the new arrivals and little shelter. The English were suspicious of the new Catholic arrivals. The three groups had little in common and fought among themselves. They were not used to the hot Florida weather and had no knowledge of growing sugar. The Minorcans fled to St. Augustine, where they settled, and others returned to their homelands.

5

THE AMERICAN REVOLUTION

Britain acquired Florida as a result of the French and Indian War, which created huge debts. One way to pay the bills was to make the colonies pay for their own protection through taxes, something the colonists balked at unless they gained a say in the operation of the government. Relations between the colonies and England began to deteriorate, except in Florida.

East and West Florida remained loyal to King George throughout the American Revolution. The taxes the king sought to impose were not a burden in Florida. The quartering act was despised in the North, where colonists were required to provide shelter, food and even a ration of liquor for British soldiers. But on the Florida frontier, where there were few soldiers and many threats—whether from the Indians, the Spanish, the French or the possibility of slave uprisings—the soldiers were welcome.

When people refer to the thirteen original colonies, they omit East Florida and West Florida. They could have sent delegates to Philadelphia but declined. While those in the thirteen northern colonies rallied around leaders like Sam Adams and John Hancock, British residents in St. Augustine burned effigies of the two men.

The non-British colonists—the Spaniards, Minorcans, French, Greek and Italians—had no desire to link with the largely Protestant colonies to the north. The Scots who had moved to Florida also remained loyal to the king.

As the American Revolution began, those in the thirteen colonies who remained loyal to King George could flee either to Canada or Florida. There was protection in either direction. England used Florida as a staging

TIMELINE 1695-1821

1695: The Spanish fort Castillo de San Marcos is completed at St. Augustine.

1702–04: British raid Spanish settlements and destroy missions.

1738: Fort Mose is established as the first free black community in what is now the United States.

1740: British invade Florida.

1763: Treaty of Paris ends the French and Indian War and gives Florida to the British, ending two centuries of Spanish rule.

1768: Turnbull Colony at New Smyrna is established, but it is abandoned in 1777.

1770: The Creeks—later called Seminoles—begin moving from Georgia and Alabama to Florida.

1776: Florida's colonists remain loyal to Britain during the American Revolution.

1783: Spain receives Florida as a result of the American Revolution.

1810: British occupy Pensacola, but Andrew Jackson drives them out in 1813.

1817–18: First Seminole War.

1821: The United States acquires Florida from Spain. General Andrew Jackson becomes territorial governor.

area for its troops and supplies. The giant St. Augustine fort, built by the Spanish in part to repulse the British, was turned into a prisoner-of-war camp for American revolutionaries. Three signers of the Declaration of Independence—Thomas Heyward Jr., Arthur Middleton and Edward Rutledge—were captured by the British and held in St. Augustine until 1781.

Hundreds of settlers flooded into St. Augustine, swelling the population and setting off a construction boom.

While England remained in firm control of East Florida, there were problems in West Florida. Indians trying to escape the war poured into the colony, and the Crown removed the governor after problems developed with the military.

The Spanish were on the losing side in the French and Indian War, and it cost the nation Florida. In the American Revolution, Spain picked the winning side. To help the colonists, Spain attacked the British at Pensacola in 1781 and bombarded the city.

The British surrender at Yorktown came as a shock to Floridians. It brought an instant and dramatic increase in the population as those who had been loyal to the king in the thirteen colonies flooded into Florida.

The thirteen colonies knew that a treaty with England would result in their independence while the Florida colonists had no idea what awaited them.

The Loyalists who escaped to Florida and those already residing there were in for a terrible surprise when the Treaty of Paris ended the war. As part of the peace settlement, Britain agreed to return Florida to Spain.

When Britain had acquired Florida in 1763, it saw it as rounding out its control from Canada to the Florida Keys. Instead, Florida became an isolated outpost of no value to the British—a financial drain.

While the British abandoned Florida, it did not abandon the Florida Loyalists. Thousands accepted the offer to move to another British colony and money to start a new life. Some went only a short distance, to the Bahamas or Jamaica, while others traveled to Canada or England. For many of the Florida residents, the return of the Spanish was a trip back in time; the Spanish and others who had come before the British period were pleased with the turn of events.

6

SPAIN RETURNS

When Britain took over Florida in 1763, the Spanish left quickly. The British, however, took their time departing. The British thought the American experiment with democracy might come crashing down, and they wanted to be close to reclaim the colonies.

By the spring of 1785, the Spanish were back. Florida had never been a moneymaker for Spain, and now an even weaker Florida gave Spain one more thing to worry about.

The Spanish tried to lure people to the colony. The Spanish governor Vicente Manuel de Zéspedes offered tax breaks, major land grants and even cash. Finally, he dropped the requirement that the settlers be Catholic and allowed more slaveholders to move in.

The changes were of little help, as few new residents came. The biggest obstacle was the Spanish trade policy that forbade trade with the United States, which would have been a major market for Florida's orange and rice crops.

West Florida did prove to be a draw for fur trappers, who found abundant game in the woods. The Spanish permitted the trading firm Panton, Leslie, and Company to establish a fur-trading business in West Florida with offices in Pensacola and Apalachicola. In East Florida, the firm of Forbes and Company received a Spanish contract for the fur trade. British Loyalists founded both firms.

Another problem was along Florida's borders with the neighboring United States. In West Florida, the boundaries had always been poorly defined. The British had initially agreed to Spain's claim that the border was at thirty degrees north latitude, but American frontiersmen wanted the land

ANDREW JACKSON

Floridians liked Andrew Jackson, naming one of the largest cities and a county in North Florida for him. Jackson did not return those feelings, spending as little time in Florida as possible and usually creating national and even international incidents when he became involved in Florida affairs.

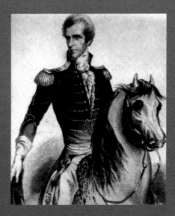

Jackson's first involvement in Florida came in 1813 against the Creek Indian Nation. When the Indians killed nearly 250 settlers in Alabama and Florida, Jackson was called to stop them. He suppressed the Indians and forced them into Spanish Florida.

Andrew Jackson was Florida's first territorial governor, but he stayed just a few months. *Florida Archives Photographic Collection.*

Jackson's actions at the Battle of New Orleans made Jackson a national hero and began to stir talk of a potential presidential campaign. He was named the military commander of most of the southeastern United States, and in 1817, he was called to respond when the Seminoles attacked across the border from Spanish Florida. President James Monroe ordered Jackson to handle the situation, but the instructions were not clear—perhaps on purpose. Jackson interpreted the orders as giving him authority to invade Spanish Florida.

Jackson captured St. Marks in the panhandle and executed four men—two Indians and two British citizens—and captured the Spanish governor. Jackson stirred protests in Washington and London, and Monroe disavowed Jackson's actions.

In 1821, Monroe offered Jackson the governorship of the Florida Territory, and Jackson resigned from the army. He did not stay long, getting into squabbles with just about everyone. He drew criticism for his dictatorial actions and ignored instructions from Washington. Most troubling for Jackson was that his wife's health declined in the Florida climate. By August, he thought of resigning, but he waited until October to quit.

and ignored the border. Spain was in no position to defend its claims. There was also trouble along the East Florida border with Georgia.

With Spain back in possession, Florida once again became a haven for runaway slaves. Indians and criminals found they could strike into Georgia, commit their crimes and steal back across the border to the safety of Spanish Florida.

Just a year after it reacquired Florida, Spain clashed with the United States over the Mississippi River. Spain closed the port of New Orleans to American ships, harming the economy of the United States and leading to threats of invasion. In 1795, the two sides agreed to negotiate, and American vessels gained access through Spanish New Orleans. This reduced demands for the seizure of Florida, but only temporarily, and Spain's rule continued to be uneasy.

The situation became worse in 1803, when the United States acquired the Louisiana Territory from France. Napoleon had taken New Orleans from the Spanish and then sold it to raise money for his military operations. The American purchase hurt Spain in two ways. First, it separated Spain's Florida territory from Mexico. Second, once again, the borders were poorly defined—Thomas Jefferson even tried to claim that West Florida was part of the purchase—and Americans rushed to take advantage of the situation.

In Washington, the demands of southerners to purchase or seize Florida grew louder, and there were attempts to buy it in 1803 and 1805. In 1810, a small group of Americans captured Baton Rouge—then part of Florida—and established what they called the Republic of West Florida. They even tried unsuccessfully to capture Mobile. President James Madison used the seizure to annex the area into the territory of Orleans.

In East Florida, a group of Georgians invaded Florida to establish the Republic of East Florida. Each member of the group was to receive two hundred acres in Florida. They headed for St. Augustine, destroying Spanish plantations along the way. Only the intervention of the British fleet saved St. Augustine.

Florida was becoming more of a liability for Spain, a haven for criminals and pirates, and the bills kept piling up—money Spain did not want to pay.

The War of 1812 was another setback for Spain. This time, Spain aligned itself with England and allowed the British to use Florida as a staging ground to fight the United States. Britain was even allowed to build a fort on the Apalachicola River.

The Red Stick Creek and Seminole Indians crossed over from West Florida into Alabama. In 1814, Jackson defeated the Indians at Horseshoe Bend.

Jackson moved into Florida to stage an unauthorized raid, which led to calls for his removal from command. He attacked Pensacola, imprisoned

A RASCAL IN FLORIDA

For a brief time, it appeared as though General Sir Gregor MacGregor might become the ruler of Florida.

Although Florida was officially a possession of Spain, the Spanish Empire was crumbling. While the Spanish maintained forts in St. Augustine, Pensacola and Amelia Island, everywhere else was up for grabs.

MacGregor, who had fought with Simón Bolívar in the liberation of Venezuela, saw an opportunity. He thought he could take Florida and sell it to the highest bidder.

Amazingly, his scheme almost worked.

He raised money in the United States by promising investors a share of the profits and recruited a ragtag army of 150 soldiers. Without firing a shot, he seized Fort San Carlos on Amelia Island. MacGregor quickly raised his green cross flag over the fort.

Almost immediately, he faced a series of problems. He ran out of money and nearly half his soldiers deserted. To help raise money, he opened the port at Amelia Island to pirates and began attacking plantations around Amelia Island.

The Spanish assembled an army of three hundred men to retake Amelia Island, and MacGregor decided it was a good time to get out. The French pirate Louis Aury arrived in the port, and MacGregor sold him the fort for $50,000. Aury set up his own kingdom, ruled by pirates and a haven for slave smugglers. He flew the Mexican flag, but his empire lasted just a few months before the U.S. Navy showed up and reclaimed the island. President Monroe said he was holding the island "in trust for Spain."

Spanish officials, frightened the British fleet into leaving the port and was about to claim all of Florida. The Spanish were saved for the moment by the British activity near New Orleans. Jackson left Florida for New Orleans, where he defeated the British.

The War of 1812 was fought to a draw, but the treaty contained negative consequences for Spain. The Spanish relied on the British navy to safeguard Florida's east coast, and with the British withdrawal, the coast was wide open to adventurers. One of those was Gregor MacGregor, who captured the town of Fernandina with hopes of establishing his own country.

By 1817, the problems in Florida became acute. American settlers were moving onto claimed land, slaves were fleeing from plantations in the United States to freedom in Florida and attacks by Florida Indians into the United States were becoming bolder.

Two British citizens, Alexander Arbuthnot and Robert Armbrister, began selling guns to the Seminoles and calling for them to fight for their land. In 1818, President Monroe ordered Jackson to go to Florida. The orders were ambiguous, perhaps intentionally by Monroe. Jackson thought he was being sent to take Florida. With two thousand troops, he seized St. Marks, executed the two British subjects and then headed for Pensacola, where he took the town, arrested two Spanish officials and set up a new government. He then left for his home in Nashville. Monroe, facing international pressure, denied he had sanctioned the invasion. The American people supported Jackson, and the attack enhanced his growing reputation.

In 1819, Secretary of State John Quincy Adams offered the Spanish a deal: trade Florida for a portion of Texas that the United States claimed as part of the Louisiana Purchase. Spain rejected the offer, but two years later, it accepted. Throughout Latin America, Spain's colonial system was starting to collapse, and Spain had larger concerns than Florida. Spain agreed to sell Florida for $5 million, leaving after nearly three hundred years. Even the $5 million figure was misleading as the money was to settle claims by Americans against Spain.

7

THE FIRST AFRICAN AMERICANS

Although they were seldom included in the early writings, Africans were present from some of the earliest explorations of the New World. The Spanish system of slavery was far different from the British system. Spanish customs and laws gave the Africans rights and protections that the British did not. Backed by the Catholic Church, the Spanish recognized slaves as human beings, not just property. This led to communities of free blacks in Spain and the New World.

Ponce de León brought the first Africans to North American in 1513 with his expedition. An attempt by the Spanish to settle on the coast of what is now Georgia included the first Africans, probably artisans rather than field workers. The settlement ended in disaster, with the remnants of the Spanish colony limping back to the Caribbean while some of the Africans seemed to have remained behind with the Indians.

Pánfilo de Narváez brought Africans in his 1528 expedition that landed around Tampa. His mission also failed, and only a handful of the original six hundred survived, including one African slave, Estevan.

Pedro Menéndez brought slaves—probably four dozen—when he settled St. Augustine. Many melted into the forests surrounding St. Augustine and lived with the Indians. The number of slaves gradually increased, and by the seventeenth century, they could be found quarrying coquina, overseeing cattle, working in homes and laboring in fields.

There were also communities of free blacks, including Fort Mose, a settlement for escaped slaves from the British colonies.

FORT MOSE

Although the Spanish enslaved native peoples in the lands they conquered, their form of slavery was less cruel than that practiced by the British in North America. Spanish slaves had rights, including the right to sue their owners and the right to petition the king over mistreatment. The Spanish government granted freedom to slaves escaping from the British colonies if they converted to Catholicism and served in the militia.

Florida became the perfect sanctuary for slaves living on plantations in Georgia and South Carolina.

In 1686, the Spanish raided an English plantation and announced that slaves could find religious sanctuary in St. Augustine. The slaves began arriving the next year—eight men, two women and an infant. King Charles II of Spain issued a Royal Proclamation "giving liberty to all the men and the women so that by their example and by my liberality others will do the same."

Many of the slaves fleeing to Florida lived with the Creek and Seminole Indians.

Research by historian Jane Landers found that by 1738, more than one hundred escaped slaves arrived, and Florida's Spanish governor Manuel Montiano set aside land outside St. Augustine to create Gracia Real de Santa Teresa de Mose, which became known as Fort Mose. The men at the fort organized a militia and vowed to fight for Spain against England.

St. Augustine was already a target for the English, and now they had another reason to attack St. Augustine and destroy Fort Mose—to discourage slaves from escaping. In 1740, Georgia governor James Oglethorpe attacked St. Augustine and destroyed Fort Mose. The escaped slaves fought bravely and, after the battle, moved into St. Augustine.

A second fort was built on the Fort Mose site in 1752. This fort was larger than the first. It had three sides and was made of earth and surrounded by a moat. It was abandoned in 1763, when England took control of Florida, and many of the fort's residents moved to Cuba.

When the British took control of Florida in 1763, they brought with them an entirely new system of slavery. The British established large plantations dependent on slavery. The British viewed slaves as property to be bought and sold with no legal rights and who could be punished by death.

The return of Florida to Spain at the end of the war complicated an already confusing situation. Some slaves were evacuated by the British while others fled to live with the Seminoles. Some slaves appealed to the new Spanish government, and at least 251 won their freedom.

Under the Spanish, the number of escaping slaves increased along with the number of freed blacks. In 1786, 27 percent of the population was black—free and slave—and by 1814, the percentage had doubled.

Slaves from Georgia, Alabama and the Carolinas escaped their plantations into Florida and freedom. The United States complained forcefully about the Spanish refuge for slaves, and in 1790, Spain gave in and agreed to return escaped slaves to their owners. Those slaves who had already won sanctuary could remain free.

When Spain turned Florida over to the United States, the agreement provided that the rights of free blacks be respected while others moved to Cuba with the help of the Spanish government.

8

THE TERRITORY
OF FLORIDA

In 1821, Florida became part of the United States, although few thought the new territory would ever amount to much. The United States acquired it primarily to get rid of the Spanish and the problems associated with that nation's fading empire.

Andrew Jackson became provisional governor because he knew the territory and was a popular choice. Jackson thought there might be a more sinister reason: he was being mentioned as a presidential candidate in 1824 and worried that being sent to Florida was a form of exile that would take him out of the public eye. To Jackson, it was more than a coincidence that the man who appointed him, Secretary of State John Quincy Adams, would be his rival for the presidency.

He arrived in Pensacola in July 1821 and saw the red-and-gold Spanish flag hauled down for the final time, 308 years after Ponce de León first saw the peninsula.

Jackson faced a long list of problems, and as the cheers faded, he had to deal with a stack of conflicting land claims from the British, the Spanish and the Americans. Jackson was a man of action, and he hated the chores he faced, such as making sure stores stayed closed on Sundays. He also had no love for Florida to begin with.

He jailed the Spanish mayor of St. Augustine for refusing to cooperate. Most of the Spanish settlers left, with some destroying their homes in order to leave nothing for the Americans.

One advantage Jackson saw in taking the governorship was that he would be able to give his friends political jobs. However, there were few jobs to distribute,

THE LEVYS: FATHER AND SON

Two men who played a vital role in Florida's early history were father and son: Moses Elias Levy and David Levy Yulee.

Moses was born in Morocco in 1782, the son of an advisor to the sultan. He lived in the West Indies, Puerto Rico and England before settling in Florida, where he acquired 100,000 acres of land around present-day Alachua County.

Moses Levy's goal was to create a Jewish utopia. This drew interest from Jews in both the United States and Europe. He attracted fewer than two dozen refugees and encountered problems with financial panics, Indian raids and challenges to his title to the land.

Moses and his wife divorced when he was young, and David Levy spent his childhood in St. Thomas. His father sent him to a private school in Norfolk, Virginia, and urged him to choose a vocation and not attend college. As adults, the two disagreed over politics and the issue of slavery. While Moses saw his political influence decline, his son became a major force in the state.

David became an attorney, was elected to the Florida territorial legislature and went to Washington as the territorial delegate. He was also active in business, chartering the Florida Railroad, which connected Fernandina Beach with Cedar Key.

David became the state's first senator after he changed his name to David Yulee, taking his grandfather's name. He became the first Jewish member of the U.S. Senate.

In 1851, he was defeated in a controversial election and then was returned to the Senate in 1855. He resigned to join the Confederate Congress. After the war, he was imprisoned for nine months and then retired to Washington, D.C.

and officials in Washington wanted to fill those jobs. Jackson submitted his resignation to President Monroe on October 21—effective at the end of the year. He didn't wait until the effective date or to receive President Monroe's letter asking that he remain before heading back to his plantation in Tennessee.

Jackson's actions in Florida created political feuds that remained after his departure. Jackson aligned himself with Richard Keith Call, who became

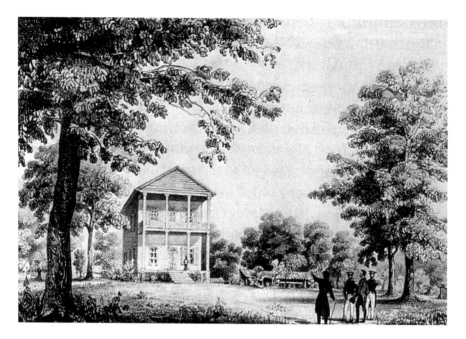

Florida's second capitol building in Tallahassee replaced three buildings made of logs.
Florida Archives Photographic Collection.

the first territorial representative to Congress, while the second group, including future senator David Levy Yulee, led the opposition.

Call's group represented the plantation owners and moneyed interests, while Levy Yulee represented the frontiersmen. The collapse of a Pensacola bank backed by Call hurt him and boosted Levy Yulee.

A plantation system developed in the rich soil around Tallahassee—known as Middle Florida—and that meant an influx of slaves. Seventy percent of the Florida slaves lived in a five-county area. The state's economy was based on slavery and cotton and was controlled by the plantation owners. Most of the settlers were small farmers who built their homes out of logs and used pieces of cloth instead of windows. Even though they did not own slaves, most supported slavery.

During this period, there were three towns of significance: St. Augustine, Pensacola and Key West.

Tallahassee became the capital as the result of a disastrous decision to have capitals in both St. Augustine and Pensacola. The original plan was to split the legislative sessions—one year in St. Augustine, the next in Pensacola. The first session in Pensacola was to begin on June 10, 1822, but a quorum

EARLY POLITICS

If there was a politician who symbolized early Florida, it was Richard K. Call. He first came to Florida in 1813 to fight the Creek Indians and drew the attention of General Andrew Jackson. A year later, he was named Jackson's personal aide and returned to Florida in 1821 to help him set up the territorial government.

He acquired a huge plantation and purchased scores of slaves, and in 1836, he was named territorial governor by President Andrew Jackson. He was replaced by Jackson's successor, President Martin Van Buren.

Even though Florida was not yet a state and could not vote in the presidential election, Call switched parties and endorsed a Whig, William Henry Harrison. His reward was another term as territorial governor, although it also earned him the dislike of many voters who never forgave him for switching parties.

When Florida became a state, Call lost to the Democratic nominee, William Moseley. The voters did elect a Whig in the next election, Thomas Brown, who is more famous for inventing the post office box than for his politics.

Democrats recaptured the governorship in 1852 and held it until 1868, when Reconstruction forced the party from power.

did not gather until July 22. Everyone realized that the traveling time was too great—and dangerous—and a search was launched for a new capital. A spot in the panhandle exactly halfway between St. Augustine and Pensacola was chosen—Tallahassee. The Seminole Indians who lived on the land were forced to move to make way for the capital.

Jacksonville began as a small settlement near Cowford (a low point in the river where the cows could cross) on the St. Johns River. It started as a boat transfer station and became a major shipping and commerce station. The Jacksonville port was important for a growing industry known as naval stores. North Florida produced lumber, tar, pitch, turpentine and resin in large quantities—all vital products in building and maintaining ships.

The naval stores industry and cotton growth were held back by the lack of a railroad. The desire to increase business meant railroads were needed.

In 1831, Florida's first railroad was chartered, a primitive twenty-two-mile, mule-drawn tram to connect Tallahassee with Port Leon on the gulf. It allowed hundreds of thousands of bales of cotton to be shipped to eastern ports. Two other railroads followed, one from Jacksonville to Lake City and another from Fernandina to Cedar Key.

At the same time, a Florida dream began—one that would last for a century and a half. The idea was to open Florida to trade by building a canal across the peninsula. The early Spanish explorers tried and failed to find a water route across the peninsula. The canal scheme would go on in fits and starts before finally being halted by President Richard Nixon.

While the railroads were a boon to the plantation owners and businessmen, the Armed Occupation Act of 1842 proved to be a draw for settlers. The law gave 160 acres to anyone who would occupy the land and agree to defend it against Indians.

More than one thousand land grants were issued under the new law during the nine months it was in effect. The planters worried that an influx of poor farmers would vote against the interests of the wealthy, which included taxes to build roads and railroads.

9

THE STATE OF FLORIDA

Today, it might seem as if statehood would have been the goal—even the dream—of any territory. Statehood meant a chance to become an equal partner in the United States, with a star added to the flag and representatives in Washington with a vote. For admission, the population had to reach a certain level, the people had to pass a referendum, a constitution had to be written and approved by Congress and then Congress had to take a final vote.

Opposition to statehood came from those who wanted Florida admitted as two states, some in West Florida who wanted to be annexed by Alabama and those who saw a financial advantage in remaining a territory. As a territory, the United States picked up most of the costs, including the salaries of officials such as the governor, who was named by the president. The federal government also paid large costs for internal improvements, such as roads. Joining the Union meant a greater voice in government, but it also meant higher taxes.

Iowa voters considered the money when they became eligible for statehood in 1840. The citizens rejected joining the Union by a three-to-one margin. Two years later, they again rejected joining the Union.

Florida's journey to statehood began in 1837, when the planters pushed for a special census to see if there were enough people for statehood, and the voters agreed to establish a constitutional convention.

When the convention met in St. Joseph to write the constitution, there was disagreement between the planters and the small farmers over banks and

CEDAR KEY

Cedar Key is a rustic, charming village on the Gulf of Mexico coast between Tallahassee and St. Petersburg. At one time, Cedar Key was on its way to becoming a major Florida city.

Cedar Key began in the 1840s as a small resort, growing after 1860 when the railroad—the state's first—reached it and connected it with the East Coast at Fernandina.

The area was named for the huge stock of cedar trees in the area, and soon the village was discovered by the pencil king Eberhard Faber, who purchased large tracts of land to supply his New Jersey pencil factory. He set up a sawmill to process the lumber.

After the Civil War, the population soared. In addition to the pencil industry, huge oyster beds and a rich stock of fish were found off the coast.

By 1889, the resources that drew people and companies were running out. No one had thought to replant the trees over the years, and the oyster beds had been cleaned out. People began moving out, and within a decade, the population was down to fewer than one thousand people.

railroads. What emerged was a document similar to that of other southern states with a decidedly anti-bank tone. Florida, like the rest of the nation, was entering an economic slump, and feelings against bankers ran high. By 1845, Florida did not have a single solvent bank.

The constitution was approved by a narrow margin on January 11, 1839, but Florida did not become a state until 1845.

A new star was added to the flag, which became four rows of stars—three with seven stars and one with six.

Florida became the last state east of the Mississippi, and William Moseley was elected as the first governor. Moseley was inaugurated under a flag with five stripes—orange, blue, red, white and green—with an American flag in the upper left-hand corner and the words "Let Us Alone" boldly printed. The words were deemed too controversial, and a new flag was ordered.

David Levy Yulee, who had fought so long for statehood, was elected to the U.S. Senate—the first Jewish senator. The population according to the

1850 census showed Florida had grown to have a total of 87,445 people with 39,000 slaves and 1,000 free blacks. It was the smallest state in the South, dwarfed by Virginia with more than 1 million and neighboring Georgia with nearly that many.

When the first session of the legislature opened, many of the legislators wore black armbands in honor of Andrew Jackson, who had just died.

10

ESTABLISHING EDUCATION

When Florida became part of the United States in 1821, land was set aside to finance and maintain public schools. For ten years, there were no public schools, primarily because of the opposition of wealthy planters. They sent their children to the few private schools in the state or to schools in Charleston, Savannah or even Europe. They saw no reason to educate the children of other families, calling public schools "pauper schools."

In 1823, Florida enacted legislation to create two institutions of higher learning—schools that would eventually become the University of Florida and Florida State University.

In 1831, an attempt to open private schools in St. Augustine and Tallahassee failed. Finally, in 1839, the territorial government came up with a system of public schools over the strong opposition of the planters who did not want to pay for schools for the poor.

The new plan produced no new schools, and another attempt in 1844 also failed. Finally, the legislature approved a lottery to pay for schools, and two were started. By the time Florida became a state in 1845, there were only a handful of public schools in its boundaries.

While a true state school system was created in 1849, progress in opening schools was slow. The 1868 constitution created a state board of education. Counties were required to collect tax money, and schools began to open. The former Confederates hated the new constitution.

Not only did the wealthy not like the plan for public schools, but the very poor also saw little value in learning. Those who did often faced the economic

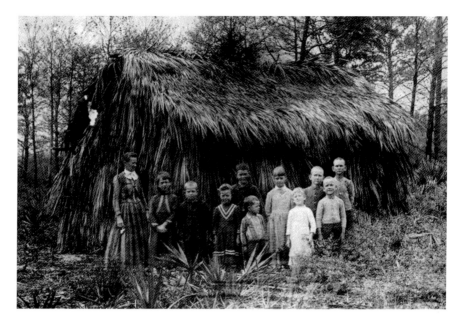

A school made of palmetto thatch in the 1890s. *Florida Archives Photographic Collection.*

reality of needing extra hands to work in the fields. It was not until 1919 that the state passed laws requiring attendance and set requirements for schools.

The post–World War II population boom brought new demands on the school system and calls for new requirements and financing. In 1957, the state created a statewide junior college system. Many of those junior colleges became four-year colleges half a century later.

In 1977, a system of statewide testing was established, which was often controversial. Beginning around 2000, it became the subject of protests by parents and educators who said that there was too much testing.

Florida schools remained segregated until the 1960s, and while all schools were sorely underfunded, African American schools were even worse off. Teachers in African American schools were paid far less than their white counterparts, and the school year was shorter, with frequent breaks to allow the students time to work in the fields for white farmers.

In 1954, the U.S. Supreme Court handed down the *Brown v. Board of Education* decision, which ordered schools to be integrated with all deliberate speed. The nine justices of the court might have felt that all deliberate speed meant quickly while Florida officials—along with their counterparts in other southern states—were able to find creative ways to delay integration.

Teaching in Florida

Susan Sanders finished training to be a teacher in Iowa in 1897, and at the age of twenty-one, she moved to the raw frontier of Palm Beach. She taught in a one-room schoolhouse and received forty dollars a month. Local women sold quilts to raise the $200 to buy lumber for the school, and their husbands built it.

Some of the teachers were as young as sixteen, about the same age as some of the students.

Hattie Carpenter came to Miami in 1900, when the town was just four years old, and was hired even though she was sure she had failed the examination: "I took the examination that spring and I guess I had the lowest grade ever given any human being down there... Somehow they gave me a certificate. I don't think I deserved it."

She quit after just three years and became a reporter for the *Miami Metropolis.*

The legislature passed a resolution claiming that the Supreme Court lacked the right to make such a decision and pronounced it null and void.

School districts throughout the state found ways to delay implementing the Supreme Court decision—dragging out the process into the next decade. Gradually, usually under the threat of legal action, school boards began to integrate.

When African American students were admitted, there was usually an exodus of white students. When four African American children at the Orchard Villa Elementary School in Miami showed up, there were only fourteen white students. The other whites began attending all-white private schools.

11

THE SEMINOLE WARS

As the population of Florida increased, so did problems with the Indians. As early as 1704, problems with the Indians began when the British allied with the Creek Indians to invade Florida. The Creeks stayed and later allied with the British in the American Revolution.

With the arrival of the British in 1763, relations with the Florida Indians declined. The settlers who came during the British era thought the Indians were in the way, occupying lands they wanted.

Even before the United States acquired Florida, the first of three Seminole Indian Wars broke out. The start of the war is in dispute; some say it began in 1814, others in 1816 or 1817 and still others in 1818. On and off, the three wars lasted until 1858.

The trouble began during the Creek War of 1813–14, when Andrew Jackson forced the Creeks to surrender much of the tribe's territory in Georgia and Alabama, forcing them into Spanish Florida. In the War of 1812, the British sought Indian allies to fight the Americans. When the war ended, the British evacuated a fort at Prospect Bluff in the Florida Panhandle, leaving it in the hands of fugitive slaves and Seminole Indians. It became known as the "Negro Fort."

In 1816, American troops invaded Florida. Relations took another turn for the worse when the United States acquired Florida. The U.S. Army attacked the Negro Fort, killing most of the 320 people in the fort. When the shooting stopped, the fort was destroyed.

As it became clear that Spain lacked the strength to police its territory, more and more people began moving to Florida and taking land from the

CHIEF OSCEOLA

In 1830, Congress passed the Indian Removal Act, which called for Indians to be moved from Florida to Arkansas and Oklahoma. At a meeting between Indians and federal officials, one young Indian leader stepped forward and plunged his knife into the document. As he stabbed the document, he said, "The only treaty I will execute is with this!" His name was Chief Osceola.

He and his followers were a nightmare for government troops, attacking and then vanishing into the swamps. Osceola agreed to meet with General Thomas Jesup under a flag of truce, unaware that Jesup had a trick up his sleeve. When Osceola showed up to talk, Jesup took him into custody.

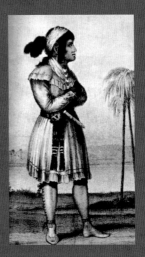

While imprisoned by the U.S. Army, Chief Osceola posed for this portrait. *Florida Archives Photographic Collection.*

Even though Osceola had been attacking U.S. troops, Jesup was widely criticized for arresting Osceola under a flag of truce.

Congress ordered an investigation, and Jesup spent the rest of his life defending his actions.

Osceola was imprisoned in St. Augustine and then was moved to Charleston, South Carolina, where he died from inflammation of the tonsils. He dressed in his finest warrior clothes, shook hands with the Indians in his party, folded his hands across his chest, smiled and died.

After Osceola's death, army doctor Frederick Weedon cut Osceola's head off and preserved it. The head ended up in a medical museum in New York, where it was destroyed by fire in 1866.

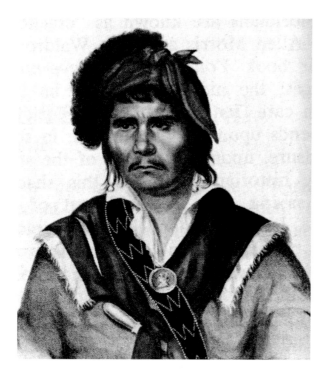

Left: Neamathla, an Indian chief in Tallahassee, was a "shrewd, penetrating man." *Florida Archives Photographic Collection.*

Below: A Seminole Indian family pose near Miami in 1929. *Florida Archives Photographic Collection.*

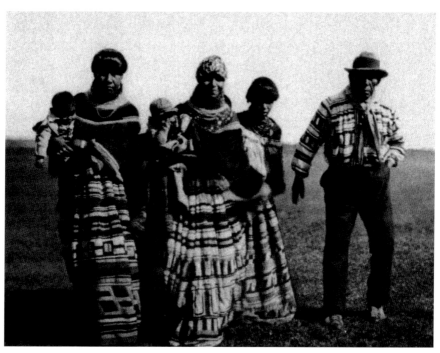

Seminoles and stealing their cattle. Soon, the Seminoles began to retaliate by raiding into Georgia. The situation escalated, and American troops began staging raids into Florida.

Secretary of War John C. Calhoun ordered Andrew Jackson to invade Florida. Jackson gathered his forces, which included nearly 1,400 friendly Lower Creek warriors, and entered Florida along the Apalachicola River. They burned the Indian town of Tallahassee and destroyed more than three hundred homes. Jackson seized a Spanish fort at St. Marks and captured Alexander Arbuthnot, a Scottish trader who had worked with the Indians, and Robert Ambrister, who claimed to be a British agent. Jackson executed the two. He also executed two Indian leaders.

Jackson then turned to Pensacola, where he exchanged cannon fire with the Spanish, forcing them to surrender a nearby fort.

Jackson's attacks came as Secretary of State John Quincy Adams was negotiating with Spain to purchase Florida. Spain suspended the negotiations but was too weak to take action against the United States. Everyone realized that the only solution would be for the United States to acquire Florida.

Relations with the Indians became worse when the United States took control. In 1823, Congress approved the Treaty of Moultrie Creek, which set aside nearly four million acres for the Indians—much of the land from Ocala to Charlotte Harbor.

Territorial governor William Duval joined negotiations with the Indians. One of the Indians at the meeting was Neamathla, who was a Seminole leader and had fought the army. During peace talks in 1823, he told Duval, "Ever since I was a small boy I have seen the white people steadily encroaching upon the Indians, and driving them from their homes and hunting grounds. I will tell you plainly, if I had the power, I would tonight cut the throat of every white man in Florida."

The focus of Indian relations shifted from Florida to Washington with the inauguration of President Andrew Jackson. If ever the Indians had an enemy, it was Jackson. He pushed through the Indian Removal Act in 1830, which called for all Indians east of the Mississippi River to be moved—by force if necessary—to the West. The agreement made both the settlers and the Indians unhappy. The Indians were slow to move to the new lands, and even before they moved, the settlers already were pushing for the Indians to be moved farther and farther west.

Sixteen years after the first Seminole War ended, the second began. The first war lasted for five years, the second for seven.

TIMELINE 1824-1887

1824: Tallahassee established as territorial capital.

1830: First steamboats bring tourists and supplies to Florida.

1834: First railroad begins operations in Florida.

1835–42: Second Seminole War brings about establishment of reservations for Florida Indians.

1837: Future president Zachery Taylor commands troops against the Seminoles at Lake Okeechobee.

1845: Florida is admitted to the Union as the twenty-seventh state.

1851: Dr. John Gorrie patents an ice-making process.

1856–58: Third Seminole War ends. Nearly all the Seminoles are removed from Florida.

1861–65: Florida joins the Confederate States of America.

1868: Florida readmitted to the Union.

1878: Tourism begins at Silver Springs with the arrival of steamboats.

Talks ultimately shifted to moving the Indians to what became known as Indian Territory in Oklahoma. In 1832, a meeting was held at Payne's Landing on the Oklawaha River. Unlike the negotiations for the Treaty of Moultrie Creek, only a few Indian chiefs showed up. Those who showed up agreed to leave Florida. The chiefs who did not attend were against moving and would not recognize the agreement.

General Wiley Thompson, the Indian agent assigned to Florida, met with the Indian chiefs who had boycotted the Payne's Landing meeting and told them that if they did not move on their own, they would be removed by force. He set a deadline for their move for January 1, 1836.

While several chiefs agreed to join those who had already decided to leave, others resisted. The leader of the Indians who refused to go was Chief Osceola. In December 1835, the Indians who had decided to depart began gathering near present-day Tampa. Meanwhile, Osceola was assembling Indians to fight.

On December 28, 1835, Thompson and an aide were killed near Fort King, located near present-day Ocala. The same day, forty miles away, Indians attacked two companies of soldiers commanded by Major Francis Dade. In the fighting near Bushnell, 108 soldiers died, and just three managed to escape. The battle became known as the Dade Massacre, and a year later, a county was named for him.

As historian Andrew Frank wrote, Osceola received the blame—or credit—for the Indian attacks, although he could not have been everywhere he is thought to have been. Osceola was not a Seminole, although his exact heritage is murky. He is believed to have been the son of a white man and a Creek mother, although some believe both of his parents were Indians.

During the Second Seminole War, there were battles nearly everywhere the settlers lived. Fighting took place as far south as Key Biscayne and even in the Everglades.

In October 1837, the army commander Thomas Jesup arranged for a meeting with Osceola under a flag of truce to discuss ending the fighting. Instead, Osceola was taken prisoner and moved to Fort Moultrie in South Carolina with nearly two hundred other Indians. He died there in January 1838.

The war continued, mostly in small battles, with the Indians striking and vanishing into the forests. Gradually, the Indians were being driven farther south until most were around the Everglades

In May 1841, Colonel William Worth was put in charge of U.S. troops. He launched a summer campaign against the Seminoles and destroyed their stronghold in the Cove of the Withlacoochee. About 300 Indians finally agreed to move, and in May 1842, President John Tyler told Congress that only about 240 Indians remained in Florida—primarily in the Everglades. He declared the war to be over. "Further pursuit of these miserable beings by a large military force seems to be as injudicious as it is unavailing," Tyler said.

The Second Seminole War left 1,500 soldiers dead, primarily from disease. No one knows how many Indians died, but more died from starvation or disease than in battle. A number of civilians died as well.

The end of the Second Seminole War brought peace, although tensions remained high, and Florida officials pushed for the removal of all the Indians from Florida. In 1849, four Indians attacked a farm near Fort Pierce, and many settlers in the surrounding area fled to St. Augustine. The War Department sent troops into Florida to supplement the limited number of troops it had. The soldiers were under orders to get the Indians to move from Florida.

Even though money was appropriated for bribes to convince the Indians to move west, most Indians refused to move. In 1851, General Luther Black was sent to convince the Indians to move. His offer to give $800 to every adult male and $450 to each woman and child failed.

In 1854, the United States stepped up its efforts against the Indians, starting a trade embargo, strengthening the army presence and launching the Third Seminole War. It was a series of small skirmishes until the arrival of General William Harney. He established forts across Florida and planned to capture or fight the Indians when they left the Everglades and Big Cypress Swamp.

Harney's plan showed few results, and he was transferred to Kansas. His successor declared the war to be over in 1858 and estimated there were only about one hundred Seminoles left in Florida, certainly a low estimate and clearly designed to show officials in Washington that the problem was solved.

Some of them left in 1859 while those who stayed overcame terrible living conditions and abject poverty to build a billion-dollar financial empire, which includes the Hard Rock clubs around the world.

The Indian wars helped bring settlers to Florida. In order to move troops and supplies, the army had to build roads and set up a communications network. The army outposts in Fort Myers, Fort Meade, Fort Pierce and Fort Lauderdale became cities. Fort Brooke became Tampa, and Fort Gatlin turned into Orlando.

12

THE CIVIL WAR

When Florida entered the Union, the two major political parties were the Whigs and Democrats. Florida was closely divided between the two parties—during the first dozen years, three of the four governors were Democrats. The Whigs generally included the leading businessmen and large plantation owners while the Democrats attracted the small farmers. National events were overtaking both parties, and the issue was slavery. It destroyed the Whigs, divided the Democrats badly and paved the way for a new party: the Republicans.

The Florida Whigs generally supported the Union while the Democrats became the party of states' rights. The Whigs evolved into the American Party and, in the 1857 election, came within four hundred votes of capturing the Florida governorship.

While the governor at the time, Madison Starke Perry, was a Democrat who was an outspoken critic of the North, both of Florida's senators, David Levy Yulee and Stephen Mallory, were cautious about leaving the Union. (The town of Perry is named for the governor, and the town of Starke may have been named for him; the town of Madison is not.) Former governor Richard Keith Call and Key West judge William Marvin led the effort to preserve the Union.

John Brown's raid at Harpers Ferry stirred passions on both sides, and tensions were high as the Democratic convention opened in April 1860 in Charleston. Southern delegates began to leave as soon as the convention began. In all, fifty-one Southern Democrats stormed out, beginning with the Alabama delegation and followed immediately by the delegates from Florida.

$50 REWARD!

My Boy, NIMROD, formerly owned by Dr. E. Branch, having run away from my plantation on the Hillsborough River, I offer the above reward of FIFTY DOLLARS to any person who will return him to me, or safely lodge him in jail and inform me of the fact, so that I may get him into my possession.

Nimrod is stout built, of low stature, having a downcast countenance, and a muttering way of speaking. He has a very large foot and hand for a person of his age, being about fifteen or sixteen years old. His color is that of a dark mulatto.

EDMUND JONES.

Tampa, Nov. 17. 1860.   37-tf

MR J. P. ANDREU

Left: In 1860, on the eve of the Civil War, a Tampa resident posted an advertisement offering a reward for the return of an escaped slave. *Florida Archives Photographic Collection.*

Below: The Union forces controlled the port of Pensacola during the Civil War, but the Confederates maintained a battery on the shore. As this picture shows, the Confederates wore many types of uniforms. *Florida Archives Photographic Collection.*

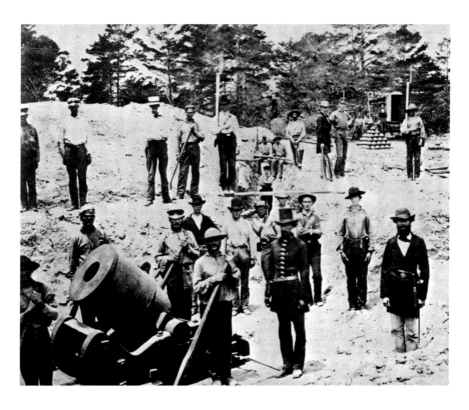

THE COURAGE OF THE FIGHTING FIFTY-FOURTH

The courage of the African American soldiers of the Fifty-fourth Massachusetts Regiment is captured in the history books and the movie *Glory*. Perhaps their greatest moment came at the Battle of Olustee. The regiment moved into Florida in early 1864 and headed toward Lake City in North Florida.

The battle with the Confederates began the next morning. Each side had about five thousand soldiers, including five hundred men from the Fifty-fourth. The battle started to go badly for the North, as the South threw all its troops into the battle while the Union commander committed his troops one unit at a time.

In the afternoon, the Fifty-fourth was ordered forward just as the other units began to fall back. As other units began to run—often dropping their guns in panic—only the Fifty-fourth held the line. They covered the retreat of the other units, and one witness said they "saved the army."

As they ran out of ammunition, they fell back in good order. Eighty-six of the five hundred men were killed or wounded. They Fifty-fourth began the 120-mile march back to Jacksonville, but the unit still had a major role to play.

A total of 1,400 Union soldiers were killed or wounded, and many were loaded on a train for the trip to Jacksonville. The train broke down, and it fell to the soldiers of the Fifty-fourth—because they were African American—to pull the train.

After the war, it was discovered that Confederate troops had murdered African American soldiers who were wounded or captured. After the battle ended, the sounds of guns being fired and soldiers' screaming could still be heard.

Even without the Southern firebrands, the convention was deadlocked. In fifty-seven attempts to get a nominee, Senator Stephen Douglas fell short of the necessary two-thirds majority. The convention gave up and reconvened in June in Baltimore. This time, 110 Southern delegates walked out, and Douglas won a worthless nomination on the second ballot. The party crumbled into three parts, allowing Abraham Lincoln to win with 40 percent of the vote because of the Democratic split.

The South went for John C. Breckinridge of Kentucky. Florida voters did not have a chance to vote for Abraham Lincoln; his name did not even appear on the ballot.

Florida voters chose John Milton as governor, who favored leaving the Union.

As soon as the November election results became clear, there were calls for Florida to leave the Union. South Carolina was the first to go, leaving in December and citing slavery as the reason for its departure. Outgoing governor Perry called a convention for January 1861, and of the sixty-nine delegates, fifty-eight were slave owners, leaving little doubt about which way the vote would go. On January 10, Florida became the third state to leave, one day after Mississippi.

Briefly, Florida became an independent nation while waiting for the Confederacy to be formed. A flag with a single star in the upper left-hand corner was raised.

Perry seized federal arms depots in St. Augustine, Fernandina and Chattahoochee, and Union forces abandoned two forts in Pensacola that were difficult to defend. The Union troops fled to nearby Fort Pickens on Santa Rosa Island.

Fort Pickens had not been occupied since the Mexican-American War and was in poor shape. The Union was determined to hold it and kept it until the end of the war. Some thought that the first battle of the Civil War would be fought over Fort Pickens—shots were fired at nearby Fort Barrancas, which was held by the Confederates—but the war began in Charleston Harbor at Fort Sumter.

Florida delegates attended a convention in Montgomery, Alabama, to form the Confederate States of America. Lincoln had not even taken office when the decisions were made.

Former territorial governor Richard Keith Call said, "You have opened the gates of Hell, from which shall flow the curses of the damned which shall sink you to perdition!"

Florida had just 140,000 residents, and 45 percent were slaves. It had the smallest population in the Union, and the number of cows outnumbered the people. A New York newspaper called it the "smallest tadpole in the dirty pool of secession."

Despite its small population, Florida sent more soldiers to the Confederate army per capita than any other state. Within the first ninety days, 6,722 men enlisted, even though the government had asked for only 5,000. The state also sent 2,350 soldiers to the Union army, almost half of them slaves.

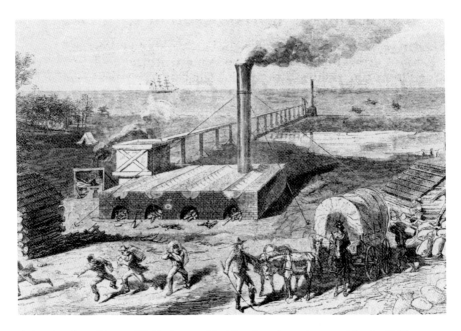

A drawing from *Harper's Weekly* shows a Florida saltworks under attack by the USS *Kingfisher*. Saltworks along the Florida coast became vital to the Confederate war effort. *Library of Congress.*

Lincoln's plan called for a Union blockade to isolate the Confederacy—known as the Anaconda Plan. Florida senator Stephen Mallory, a member of the U.S. Senate's Naval Affairs Committee who had resisted joining the Confederacy, became the Confederate secretary of the navy. He proved to be an innovative choice, building a navy from scratch to take on the Union navy and get much-needed supplies to the Confederate army. It was Mallory who oversaw the development of the ironclad. The highest-ranking officer from Florida was General Edmund Kirby Smith, who commanded what was known as the Trans-Mississippi, the vast area including Texas and known as Kirby Smithdom.

Although Florida had the longest coastline in the Confederacy, most of the navy's resources went to more important ports such as Charleston, Norfolk and New Orleans. It meant that Mallory, the Floridian, had to reject the pleas of the Florida governor for more protection for Florida ports. Florida's extensive coastline offered opportunities for smugglers bringing goods into the Confederacy. During the four years of war, 232 smugglers were stopped by Union ships while hundreds of others got through the blockade. The problem for the smugglers was that even if goods were brought ashore, they

THE CONSPIRATOR

His sister remembered Lewis Powell as "lovable, sweet, kind." Neighbors called him tenderhearted. His father thought he might spend his life doing church work. Instead, he ended up dangling from the end of a rope in the most sensational crime of the nineteenth century.

Powell was one of the men who conspired with John Wilkes Booth to kill President Abraham Lincoln, the vice president and the secretary of state. Powell was born in Live Oak, where his father was a minister. He joined the Confederate army and was wounded and captured at Gettysburg. He escaped the prison camp and rejoined the Confederates. Early in 1865, he deserted and headed north

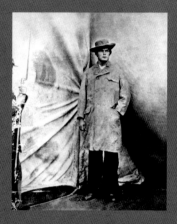

Live Oak native Lewis Powell was one of the conspirators in the Lincoln assassination. More than a century after his execution, his body was returned to Florida for burial. *Library of Congress.*

to Baltimore. There he met John Wilkes Booth, who recruited Lewis for his plot to kidnap or kill Lincoln. Lewis was recruited for his size—by the standards of 1865, he was huge at well over six feet tall.

Booth planned to kill Lincoln, and Powell was assigned to kill Secretary of State William Seward. He went to Seward's house, rushed to his bedroom and tried to stab him. Although he injured Seward, the secretary recovered.

Powell fled Seward's home and was captured when he returned to the boardinghouse where he and the other conspirators were staying. After a brief trial, he was executed with his co-conspirators before a large crowd. He was buried secretly, but more than a century later, his family had the body moved to Geneva, near Orlando.

were difficult to transport to either the soldiers or those citizens willing to pay handsomely for some luxury.

Florida was an afterthought for the Confederacy. Its location was of little significance for either side. And that meant that the state's soldiers were sent far away to die in places they had never heard of, like Shiloh, Gettysburg and Antietam.

Union gunboats surrounded the state. Key West refused to go along with succession and remained a Union stronghold. Union troops held Fort Pickens in Pensacola throughout the war despite Confederate attempts to capture it. It meant that the port of Pensacola was worthless for the Confederates. In January 1862, the Union seized Cedar Key, and two months later, Jacksonville fell.

Florida was important because of its cattle; millions of cows were desperately needed to feed the Confederate army. The Florida cows were especially valuable because they could be raised in relative safety, far away from the fighting.

The state also had salt, which was vital to the Confederacy. Salt was used to cure beef in the days before refrigeration, and it was even necessary in tanning leather to make shoes for the soldiers. Salt was as important as ammunition to the soldiers.

When the war began, it appeared that the Confederates had all the salt they needed in western Virginia. But when the people of that region formed West Virginia, the salt was lost. The Florida salt came from seawater that was boiled in large kettles, from which the salt was removed. By necessity, the salt producers were along the coast and easy targets for Union ships. Attacks were frequent, but the salt makers resumed operations quickly. There were times they were making salt again before the Union ships had sailed out of sight. More than five thousand people worked in salt making, and their work was so vital that the men were exempt from the draft.

While the state's cattlemen experienced unprecedented demand for their cattle to feed hundreds of thousands of soldiers, there was a major problem: money. Before the war, they had either shipped their cows to Cuba or sold them in the United States for gold. Cattlemen, such as Jacob Summerlin, often had saddlebags full of gold coins and were among the wealthiest men in the state. The Confederate government had little gold and paid for goods in increasingly worthless paper money. Sometimes there was not even Confederate cash, just a slip of paper from a procurement official.

The Florida cattlemen began to hide their cows, driving them to places such as Fort Myers and away from seizure. The cattlemen faced the lure of

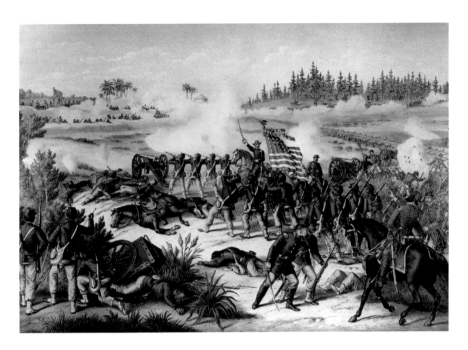

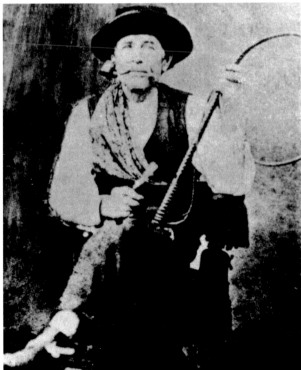

Above: This drawing shows Union soldiers fighting bravely at Olustee, but they were soon in full retreat. *Florida Archives Photographic Collection.*

Left: Jacob Summerlin created a cattle empire and became the wealthiest man in the state. *Historical Society of Central Florida, Incorporated.*

the Cuban market. A cow in Cuba went for thirty dollars in gold compared to three dollars in the South.

In Florida, the departure of fifteen thousand young men for the military—one out of five white Floridians—left those who remained in dire straits. The stores quickly ran out of nearly everything, and getting new supplies was very difficult and often impossible. Florida was a state of small farmers, and the departure of the head of the family meant that the wife, daughter or mother was left to do the work. The Union blockade forced shortages as coffee went to a dollar a pound and pork soared to fifty dollars a barrel. The smugglers grew wealthier as the people suffered.

There were fears that the slaves might rebel, but while some ran away, there was no rebellion.

There was just one significant battle in Florida—a February 1864 clash in Olustee. The reason for the invasion was political, military and economic. Florida was still supplying thousands of cattle and hogs to the Confederate army, and cutting off Florida would make the starving Southern army even hungrier. President Abraham Lincoln was trying to get Florida back into the Union so that he could pick up three electoral votes in what he thought would be a tough reelection year. And the Union presence in Florida would attract African American recruits to the Union army.

The Union army moved west from Jacksonville toward Lake City, at the time the largest city between Jacksonville and the panhandle. The Union army never made it to Lake City. Thirteen miles east of the town, Confederate forces from Georgia and Florida met the Union soldiers, halting the advance and sending the soldiers fleeing to Jacksonville. It was a rout as the Union troops ran from the field, leaving their wounded soldiers behind.

The casualty figures told the story: 93 Confederates killed and 847 wounded; 203 Union soldiers killed and 1,152 wounded. There were six Confederate soldiers missing and a staggering 506 Union soldiers unaccounted for, mostly men who had seen enough of war and disappeared into the Florida brush.

The invasion was a failure, and ended the North's effort to retake Florida.

The Battle of Natural Bridge in March 1865 was one of the final Confederate victories of the war and saved Tallahassee from capture, the only Confederate capital east of the Mississippi River not captured during the war.

As the war came to an end in 1865, Governor John Milton went to his home in Marianna, about sixty-five miles northwest of Tallahassee, with his wife and son to see firsthand the destruction of farms by Union soldiers.

While he was out of the capital, bands of Confederate deserters entered the city in an attempt to kidnap the governor. Milton proclaimed that "death would be preferable to reunion," and on April 1, he shot himself in the head.

There was yet one drama to be played out involving Florida. As General Robert E. Lee's army abandoned the defense of Richmond, the leaders of the Confederate government fled south. Just north of the Florida border, President Jefferson Davis was captured by Union troops. Secretary of War John C. Breckinridge—a former vice president of the United States—moved down the state to the Indian River and took a small boat to Cuba. Secretary of State Judah Benjamin, moved the other way, heading down the west coast and then, like Breckinridge, to Cuba. Stephen Mallory was also captured with Davis and jailed for nearly a year.

Of the fifteen thousand soldiers who left Florida to fight, five thousand did not come home. Thousands more were wounded, and hardly a family was not touched by the fighting.

13

RECONSTRUCTION

The end of the Civil War found Florida destitute. The state's entire economic system was based on slavery and Confederate money, and now both were worthless. For more than a century after Robert E. Lee surrendered at Appomattox Court House, the legacy of the Civil War haunted Florida.

It was not enough that one-third of the Confederate soldiers who marched off to war never came home; nearly another third were dead within a decade, the result of wounds and deprivations suffered during the war. Unlike their Union counterparts, the Confederate soldiers did not receive any benefits or healthcare.

The war changed Florida in many ways. Without the slaves, the large plantations could not be sustained. Many turned to sharecropping, in which smaller farmers—sometimes former slaves—grew crops and gave the plantation owner a share of the crops in lieu of rent payments. Others tried tenant farming, in which land was leased for cash or a combination of cash and crops. Many plantations and farms were seized by the tax collector. Northern investors swooped in to buy them, often for unpaid taxes. Some plantations were carved up into small farms.

Although the slaves were freed, no one knew quite what to do with them. Many wanted to get far away from the plantations where they had worked as property, and thousands headed for the cities, which were still reeling from the war and unable to cope with the influx. Briefly, the War Department considered a plan to create a Negro Territory similar to the Indian Territory of the West. All the land from Ocala to Miami would be turned over to the

JOSIAH WALLS

Josiah T. Walls was the first African American member of the U.S. House of Representatives from Florida, although he spent most of his time fighting to hold on to his seat.

Born into slavery in Virginia and forced to work for the Confederate army during the Civil War, he was captured at Yorktown, Virginia, and joined the U.S. Colored Troops, rising to sergeant. When the war ended, he was stationed in Alachua County and decided to remain there.

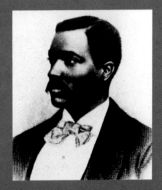

Josiah Walls became the first African American congressman from Florida, but he faced repeated election challenges. *Florida Archives Photographic Collection.*

He took a job in a sawmill and then as a teacher with the Freedmen's Bureau in Gainesville, and in 1868, he purchased a sixty-acre farm.

He was one of the few former slaves who could read and write, and he won election to the Florida Senate.

Florida had just one seat in Congress, and the Republicans gave their 1870 nomination to Walls. In the general election, he faced a Confederate veteran and won a narrow victory. The Democrats were not ready to give up and challenged the results in Congress. After Walls had been in Congress for nearly two years, Congress ruled that the Democrat was the true winner.

By 1872, Florida had two seats in Congress, and Walls once again entered the race and won one of the seats. He returned to Washington uncontested.

He won by a narrow margin in 1874 only to face another challenge. For the second time, Walls was stripped of his seat. He failed to win the nomination in 1876.

He returned to the state senate and served there through the 1879 session. By the time he died in 1905, he was forgotten, and no newspaper published his obituary.

former slaves. Nothing came of the idea, and rumors that each slave would receive forty acres and a mule were largely intended to separate the slaves from the little money they had.

African Americans made up nearly half of Florida's population of 140,000. The Freedmen's Bureau was established to help the freed slaves, and its representatives came into Florida to give advice and do their best to protect their rights. They established schools and orphanages and urged the freedmen to return to work—this time for wages—often on the plantations where they had toiled as slaves.

Florida had less damage than any state in the Confederacy except for Texas. Still, the railroad was unusable, and thousands of men came home badly wounded.

As was the situation throughout the South, politics in Tallahassee was in turmoil as the state had seven governors in nine years. When Governor John Milton committed suicide, he was replaced by Abraham Allison, who took over on April 1, 1865, the first day of the final month of the four-year war. Allison was the state senate president and never thought he would become governor. He served just forty-nine days before resigning and fleeing the capital as Union troops marched in.

He was replaced by William Marvin, who got the title "provisional governor." Marvin was a federal judge in Florida and was loyal to the Union. He was appointed to the post by President Andrew Johnson, but he served just five months before being elected to the Senate. The U.S. Senate voted to deny him a seat—as it did all the elected officials from the Confederacy—and his political career came to an end.

To replace him, the voters chose David Walker, who seemed to believe that the war was not over and the Confederates were still in charge. As required by Washington, a constitutional convention convened in 1865, which approved the Thirteenth Amendment and revoked the ordinance of succession. However, the delegates undid the good of those two actions by passing the Black Codes, severely limiting the rights of the former slaves. A special committee recommended the continuation of the "benign, but much abused and greatly misunderstood institution of slavery."

The Black Codes were dedicated to re-creating slavery and were embraced by every southern state. The codes angered Congress, which responded by extending the life of the Freedmen's Bureau, passing the Civil Rights Act of 1866 and approving the Fourteenth Amendment.

The more lenient form of Reconstruction, initially proposed by Lincoln and followed by Andrew Johnson, gave way to Radical

JONATHAN GIBBS

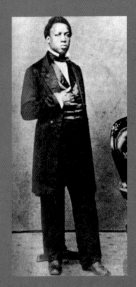

Jonathan Gibbs became Florida's first statewide African American state official. *Florida Archives Photographic Collection.*

Jonathan Gibbs was the first African American to hold statewide office in Florida, serving as secretary of state and superintendent of public instruction.

Gibbs was born in Philadelphia and trained as a carpenter. Then he studied to be a Presbyterian minister. He became involved in the abolitionist movement and worked with Frederick Douglass. He spent the war as a preacher in Philadelphia.

As the Civil War ended, he moved south to help the newly freed slaves, opening a school in Charleston. In 1867, he arrived in Florida and started a private school in Jacksonville, and he began to show an interest in politics. He was involved in writing the 1868 Florida Constitution, although his motions largely failed.

In 1868, he was named Florida's secretary of state, and in 1873, he became the first superintendent of public instruction. He was also commissioned a colonel in the state militia and elected to the Tallahassee City Council.

His post as secretary of state was largely ceremonial, but he did use the position to launch investigations into the Ku Klux Klan. The post of superintendent of public instruction was created by the Reconstruction legislature to create a public school system.

He started with very little and tried to build a school system. He standardized textbooks and set standards where there had been none. The schools had been ordered segregated by the legislature. In a state with limited financial resources, having two systems was a great burden.

Gibbs died in 1874 after giving a speech to a group of Republicans. Although there was speculation about the cause of his death, it was officially listed as a heart attack.

Reconstruction, controlled by Congress and designed to punish the South. The South was divided into five military districts. Florida was in District 3 with Georgia and Alabama. The former Confederates found themselves without political power. By April 1, 1867, Florida was under military rule, and the civilian government only had the powers the federal government allowed.

The results were fast in coming, and by 1868, the Republicans had taken control of the state legislature.

One major change was an influx of northerners who saw a chance to make their fortune in the ruins of the Confederacy. Thousands came to the state, starting businesses, buying large tracts of land and becoming involved in politics. The 1868 election brought thirteen northerners—called "carpetbaggers" by critical southerners—to the state House of Representatives. Another new presence in the legislature were African Americans (there were nineteen) and there were twenty-one white southerners who supported the Union—derisively referred to as "scalawags" by the former Confederates.

The 1868 election also produced a major shift in the governorship when Republican Harrison Reed, a native of New Hampshire, and a newcomer to Florida, was elected. Reed's term was stormy, and he managed to anger both sides with the result that there were four attempts to impeach him. Although from the North, he was no friend of the former slaves. He vetoed a bill to give blacks equal rights in hotels and railroads.

He was replaced by another Republican, Ossian Hart, the first native Floridian to be elected governor. He died within a year—under suspicious circumstances. He was replaced by his lieutenant governor, Marcellus Stearns, a Republican from Maine.

By 1876, anti-Confederate sentiment in Washington was declining. Those who led the charge in Congress to make the South pay for the Civil War were dying or retiring. The soldiers sent from the North to enforce the laws were being replaced by a new generation for whom the Civil War was just a childhood memory. By 1876, only Florida, South Carolina and Louisiana remained under Republican rule.

In Florida, the Democrats were coming back to power, and for the first time in a decade, they won back the governorship. The 1876 election was dramatic—both in Florida and throughout the nation. George Drew, a Democrat who had the backing of the old Confederates, won the governorship by a narrow margin over the incumbent, Stearns. For nearly a century, the Democrats dominated state politics.

The nation's eyes turned to Florida because it would determine the next president. On election night in 1876, Samuel Tilden, the Democratic nominee, led Republican Rutherford B. Hayes nationally by a comfortable margin in the popular vote. In the electoral vote, Tilden had 184 votes, one short of securing victory, and the results from three states were in dispute. Florida's four electoral votes would ultimately decide the next president.

Both parties sent representatives into the state to influence the results by buying election officials and promising great rewards. One of those sent to Florida was Republican operative Lew Wallace. For his reward in securing Florida votes, he was named territorial governor of New Mexico, where he found time to write his classic, *Ben-Hur.*

The southern Democrats agreed to go along with the Republican election in exchange for a guarantee to end Reconstruction. The end of Reconstruction also meant the rights the former slaves had gained began to disappear.

14

THE EARLY TOURISTS

At first they were called strangers, and since they came from the North, they became known as "Yankee Strangers." It was not until late in the 1800s that they were called tourists, a word imported from Europe and used to describe those on a "Grand Tour" of the Continent.

The first tourists came for their health, which seemed strange because Florida was wet and swampy and a breeding ground for yellow fever and malaria. Physicians sent their patients by the hundreds, with the hope of curing a long list of ailments. Many were suffering from tuberculosis, known as consumption, and marked by a hacking cough. These same doctors were wrong about the disease—they thought it was hereditary, not communicable, and could be cured by devouring enough vegetables, exercising and the Florida climate.

One of the first to come was Dr. Andrew Anderson and his wife, Mary, who suffered from consumption. Even though his wife died, Anderson remained a true believer.

A brochure promoting Orlando promised a climate that "soothes the weary mind, invigorates the enfeebled body, and finally wins the visitor."

The main attraction was St. Augustine, although it was not much of an attraction. When John James Audubon came to town in 1831 on his way to paint birds, he called it the "poorest hole in creation."

Florida's first hotel, the Florida House, opened in St. Augustine in 1835.

Outside St. Augustine, the natural springs were the big draw, and "taking the waters" was recommended by countless doctors. It was believed that the spring waters could not only cure consumption but also jaundice, dysentery, diarrhea, gout, syphilis, ringworm and a dozen other ailments.

The search for health cures began to subside by the 1890s, although it remained a factor of early tourism until the early 1900s. Instead, people began to come for the warm weather and the scenery and to see the beautiful flowers, birds and abundant wildlife. More importantly, Floridians found that wealthy visitors spent more money than the sick and dying visitors.

And for the first time, there were concerted efforts to encourage the visitors. Poet Sidney Lanier was hired by the Atlantic Coast Line Railroad to promote Florida and the railroad. Lanier, who was suffering from consumption, stressed the healthy nature of the state, although he died at the age of thirty-nine. Lanier wrote that "consumptives are said to flourish in this climate."

Harriet Beecher Stowe made her reputation and her fortune as the author of *Uncle Tom's Cabin*, the novel and play that helped galvanize the North against slavery. After the war, she bought a farm outside Jacksonville on the St. Johns River. She began writing about the beauty of Florida, and she even offered advice for buying land. Her articles were combined in a book, *Palmetto Leaves*, which sold well. Stowe herself became a tourist attraction, sitting outside her home as the steamboats passed. Eventually she built a long dock in front of her home, and there were rumors that the steamboat line paid her to come out and wave. Around 1880, guidebooks began appearing to describe the best places to visit.

The major railroads stopped in Jacksonville, and from there, visitors usually took steamboats. In 1882, seventeen thousand tourists arrived in Jacksonville either by rail or ship.

The steamboats offered every level of service, from basic transportation with no staterooms to boats with luxury salons that were comparable to the finest hotels. There were a number of cruise destinations, with most traveling the St. Johns to Palatka, which functioned much as an airline hub does today. From there, visitors could take the excursion to Silver Springs for twelve dollars or the trip to Leesburg for twenty dollars.

Where the river stopped, there were stagecoaches to continue the journey.

The real impact on Florida tourism came from two men who had already made their fortunes by the time they came to Florida. Henry Plant and Henry Flagler—sometime partners, sometime friendly foes—transformed the state. Together, they created the tourism industry in Florida.

Flagler made his fortune as John D. Rockefeller's partner at Standard Oil, although it is Rockefeller who is best remembered, even he conceded

THE STEAMBOATS

Railroads in Florida developed slowly. There were no major cities to connect, and the early railroads went between largely forgotten towns. The steamship was the primary form of transportation in Florida during most of the 1800s.

In the early 1800s, steamboats started to replace sailboats and were perfect for moving people and goods along Florida's rivers. The steamship era lasted for nearly a century.

While the St. Johns River was the center of the steamboat industry, there were ships moving along the Apalachicola River in the panhandle, the Halifax River near Daytona Beach and the Indian River near Titusville.

Although shipbuilding became a major Florida industry in the twentieth century, the steamships that plied Florida rivers in the 1800s were largely built elsewhere.

The steamships also connected Florida with the rest of the United States. The primary routes were from Jacksonville to Charleston or Savannah, which then connected to Baltimore, New York or Boston. On the state's west coast, the steamships went from Tampa to New Orleans, Mobile or Havana.

While records are sketchy, it is believed that the *George Washington* was the first steamboat to come to Florida, arriving in Jacksonville in 1827 from Savannah after a thirty-four-hour journey.

Service along the St. Johns began in the 1840s when the *Sarah Spalding*—one of the first ships built in Jacksonville—connected Jacksonville with Mellonville, now Sanford. The town of Enterprise became a major port, and even a county seat, because it was a major landing spot for the ships.

that that it was Flagler who came up with the plan to monopolize American oil production by driving or buying out their competitors. Rockefeller said, "No, sir. I wish I had the brains to think of it. It was Henry M. Flagler."

By the time Flagler came to Florida, he was one of the wealthiest men in the country. He first came to Florida in 1878 with his wife, Mary, who was in poor health. He did not enjoy Jacksonville or his trip. His wife died in

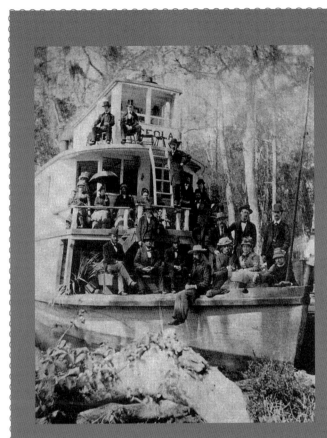

Former president Ulysses S. Grant (seated on the main deck, far left) took a steamboat ride on the St. Johns and dedicated the railroad that eventually stretched from Sanford to Tampa. *Florida Archives Photographic Collection.*

The early 1880s were the highpoint of travel on the St. Johns, but the decade also saw the beginning of the end for the steamboats. Railroads were being built at a record rate, and many of the ports along the St. Johns began to fade.

1881, and Flagler returned in 1883 for a honeymoon with his new wife. The couple discovered St. Augustine, and Flagler found a new career.

He decided to turn the small town into a resort for his wealthy friends. First he built the giant Ponce de Leon Hotel, as magnificent a hotel as anywhere in the world. Even before it opened in early 1888, he was already planning a second hotel to be built across the street. The Alcazar Hotel had more moderately priced rooms and the world's largest indoor swimming pool.

SILVER SPRINGS

Silver Springs was Florida's first attraction, a mighty spring at the headwaters of the Silver River near Ocala. Even before the Civil War, visitors were making the difficult journey to see crystal clear waters and swarming fish. After the Civil War, steamboats began bringing visitors down the Ocklawaha to see Silver Springs.

In the 1880s, a hotel was built on the shore and an enterprising businessman rented rowboats. There are many versions of the story of the glass-bottom boat. Most likely it was developed in the late 1870s or early 1880s and offered guests the chance to see the marvels beneath the surface of the water. A fleet of motorboats was added before World War I.

In 1924, two businessmen, William Ray and W.C. Davidson, bought the springs and turned them into a major attraction. They launched a major upgrading and began promoting the glass-bottom boats. They began to advertise extensively and added some additional attractions. There was Ross Allen's Florida Reptile Institute, which started as a collection of snakes and turtles from the swamps around the springs. A replica of a Seminole Indian village was added, and Native American reenactors were hired for it.

A major boost for the springs came in the 1930s, when MGM Studios went to Silver Springs to film the fourth in its *Tarzan* movies

A competitor tried to cash in on the wave of tourists by building the Casa Monica Hotel next door. But the Casa Monica's builder ran into financial problems, and within a few months, Flagler owned it also.

The hotels had an immediate impact, revitalizing a town that had become dirty and shabby. The guests who came usually stayed for what was known as "the season," those months when it was freezing in the North.

Flagler knew that he had to improve the town and spent money on new roads, schools and churches. He built the Memorial Presbyterian Church—thought to be the most expensive building for its size ever built in the United States—in memory of his daughter, Jennie, who died in 1889.

He began spending more time on his railroad, buying a handful of small railroads, at first to speed service to his St. Augustine resort. But then he saw it as starring Johnny Weissmuller. It became *Tarzan Finds a Son.* For the fifth and sixth films, MGM moved to Wakulla Springs between Tallahassee and the Gulf of Mexico.

A promoter convinced the owners to launch boat tours along the river and, to make the springs appear more jungle-like, brought in rhesus monkeys. Soon, the monkeys were everywhere. The stories that the monkeys were left over from the *Tarzan* movies are false; Tarzan and Jane hung around with chimps, not rhesus monkeys.

Tourism declined during World War II, but after the war, it exploded as families wanted to travel. Silver Springs billboards could be seen as far north as Maine. Even without Tarzan, the moviemakers still came. In 1949, *The Yearling* was filmed there and later *Distant Drums* and *Jupiter's Darling* with Esther Williams. One of the best known was the drive-in movie classic *The Creature from the Black Lagoon,* which was filmed there and at Wakulla Springs. The television show *Sea Hunt* with Lloyd Bridges was set in Silver Springs.

In 1962, ABC-Paramount purchased Silver Springs. ABC had already acquired Weeki Wachee Springs, and executives thought they were creating a tourism empire. After the opening of Disney, other older parks began to see tourism decline while Silver Springs remained strong. ABC got out of the attractions business in 1984, as the park was failing. The state of Florida acquired it in 1993.

a profitable business to add to his already huge fortune. He could leave his Fifth Avenue mansion, board his private car and head directly for St. Augustine.

He expanded the line to Daytona, stopping along the way to buy the Ormond Beach Hotel, a sprawling wooden structure that featured a golf course.

Daytona (it became Daytona Beach in 1926) and Titusville were either less than enthusiastic about Flagler's building plans or thought Flagler would be a sucker willing to pay any amount of money. He skipped them and kept moving south.

His second career became a huge business. It was no longer just about hotels and wealthy guests but also about huge land holdings and shipping fresh fruit and vegetables to markets in the North. When he reached Lake Worth, he became intrigued by a barrier island that could offer his wealthy

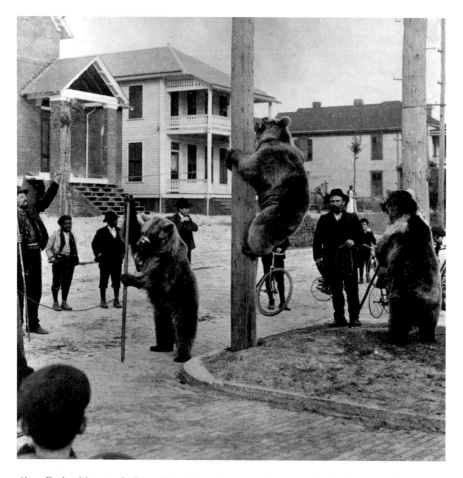

Above: Early visitors to Jacksonville gathered to see performances by the bears in downtown Jacksonville. *Florida Archives Photographic Collection.*

Opposite, top: This 1904 photo shows a horseless carriage among the horse-drawn carriages driving on Daytona Beach, a tradition that continues today. *Florida Archives Photographic Collection.*

Opposite, bottom: Henry Flagler's Ponce de Leon Hotel changed Florida when it opened in 1888. The hotel attracted some of the nation's wealthiest visitors and was the first step in the development of the state's east coast. *Collection of the author.*

guests not only a grand resort but also something more important to them—privacy. He could restrict access to the barrier island to those he deemed worthy of entry. He renamed the island Palm Beach, and on the mainland, he built West Palm Beach for those who worked on his railroad and tended to his wealthy guests on the island.

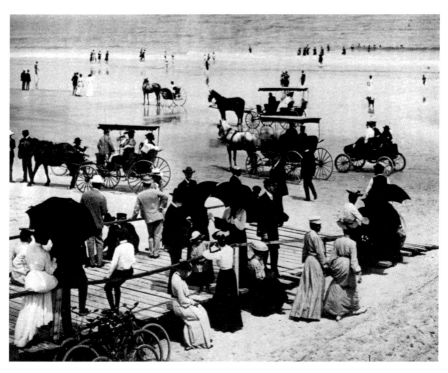

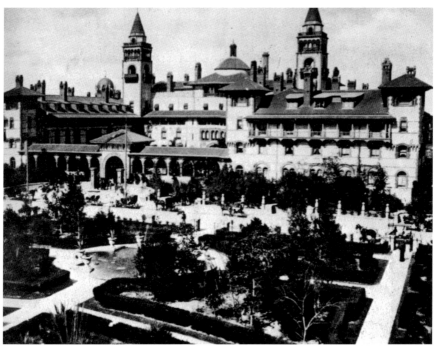

JULIA TUTTLE

Julia Tuttle was the only one who could see that Miami would one day be a great city. When she first arrived in the 1870s, there was almost nothing there. She purchased 640 acres on the north bank of the Miami River— today it is the heart of downtown Miami.

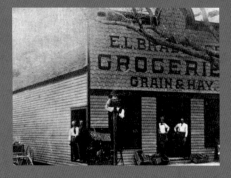

E.L. Brady's general store was one of the first buildings in Miami. This photo is from 1886 before the town was incorporated, and Henry Flagler's railroad arrived. *Florida Archives Photographic Collection.*

She hoped people would build homes, although there was not much to attract them. The heat and mosquitoes were unbearable, and the village was very difficult to reach.

Meanwhile, Henry Flagler saw the potential of Florida as a tourist mecca and a fruit and vegetable center. He had already turned St. Augustine, Ormond Beach and Palm Beach into major tourist destinations.

Tuttle needed Flagler's railroad to bring in tourists and new residents and began to lobby him. Flagler was already planning to extend his line to be able to ship more food north.

To help attract him, Tuttle offered him free land to build a hotel—the Royal Palm—and she soon thought wide streets should be laid out for the day when the village would become a major city.

Flagler could not see it. He told her, "It would be silly. This place will never be anything more than a fishing village for my hotel guests!"

In April 1896, the first trains reached Miami, and the 343 voters decided to incorporate. Unfortunately, Tuttle never lived to see her town develop; she died two years later.

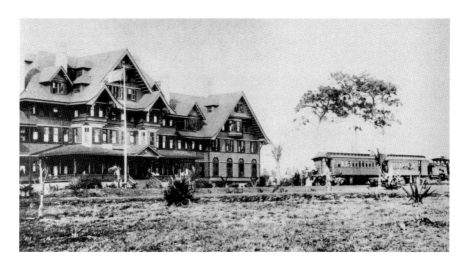

In 1907, Henry Plant built the Belleair Biltmore Hotel as a resort with a golf course. It is the last of the grand resort hotels still in operation. Millionaires pulled their private train cars in front of the hotel on Clearwater Bay. *Florida Archives Photographic Collection.*

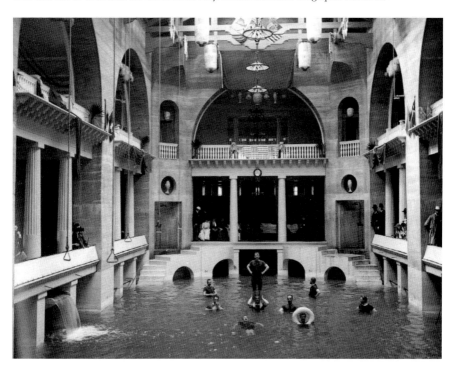

After building his massive Ponce de Leon Hotel in St. Augustine, Henry Flagler built the Alcazar Hotel across the street. It opened on Christmas Day 1888 and featured a large indoor pool. *Collection of the author.*

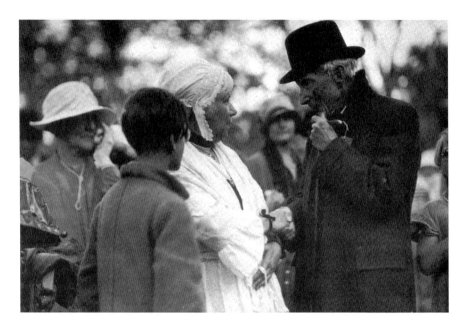

John D. Rockefeller greets visitors near his Ormond Beach home. Rockefeller purchased a home in 1918 after coming to the area for years to see his friend and business partner, Henry Flagler. *Florida Archives Photographic Collection.*

To acquire the land for Palm Beach, he used some of the ruthless business practices he had used to make his Standard Oil Company a monopoly. He also used those practices on the Florida legislature when he wanted a divorce. His second wife became mentally ill, and Flagler used his influence and his money to get a divorce. Insanity was not grounds for divorce in Florida, but Flagler was powerful enough to get the law changed. Four years after he had remarried, the legislature changed the law back again.

The Royal Poinciana Hotel had 540 rooms and every extravagance that could be imagined. The Royal Poinciana was built on the Lake Worth side of Palm Beach. Then, Flagler built his first hotel on the Atlantic Ocean, the Palm Beach Inn. Before the turn of the century, many of the wealthy avoided the beach—a suntan was a sign of a common laborer.

After he built the Palm Beach Inn, guests asked to stay at his hotel by the "breakers," or ocean. Gradually, they referred to the hotel as the Breakers.

His guests decided that building private mansions was better than staying in luxury hotels, and a building boom began. One of those who grew rich from the building boom was architect Addison Mizner, who built the exclusive Everglades Club and then turned his attention to mansions.

In 1925, he purchased seventeen thousand acres for his own version of Palm Beach, Boca Raton. His timing was terrible, and although he had major investors, the economy swamped him. By 1926, he had lost control of his development, and bankruptcy followed. His dream did become a reality when the economy recovered.

There is a wonderful story that to lure Flagler to Miami, the village's primary landowner, Julia Tuttle, sent Flagler flowers to show him that while it might be cold elsewhere, it was still warm in Miami. The flowers supposedly convinced him to extend his railroad to Miami. The fact is that as early as 1892, Flagler had obtained a charter from the state to extend his railroad to Miami.

Flagler extended his line to Miami, built another luxury hotel and then, in his boldest move, built a railroad to Key West.

Flagler is best remembered for creating the tourist industry along Florida's east coast but less remembered for creating the agricultural industry that produced tens of thousands of jobs.

If Flagler was responsible for developing the east coast of Florida, another Henry—Henry Plant—developed the west coast. Plant developed his wealth during the Civil War. Like Flagler, Plant was from the North and came south to work as the agent for the Adams Express Company, then the largest express shipping company in the nation, as the superintendent for the South. When the Civil War came, the company thought its southern holdings might be seized by the new Confederate government and transferred the southern offices to Plant.

The Confederate government used Plant's Southern Express Company for a variety of services, and by the end of the war, Plant had built an extensive company.

The war left the South in ruins. The railroads that were not torn up were often in bankruptcy. Plant began buying small, bankrupt railroads at auctions; building some new railroads; and eventually ended with more than 2,100 miles of track. He connected Georgia railroads to Jacksonville and then turned west while Flagler concentrated on the east coast. He also organized steamship lines connecting Tampa with Mobile and Havana.

He organized a holding company, and one of his investors was Flagler. In 1887, Plant built his first hotel in Sanford, the Pico Hotel, which still stands. Sanford was an early steamship and railroad hub and remains a rail center—visitors taking the Amtrak Auto Train leave from Sanford. At first he planned to build his line to Cedar Key, where local residents demanded too much money. He moved to the village of Tampa as the port for his new steamships and for the major railroad yard.

THE OSTRICH FARM

One of the first attractions in Florida was the Ostrich Farm, which opened in 1892. People paid to watch ostrich racing with jockeys dressed in silks like their horseback-riding counterparts.

Ostriches are nasty creatures, known for kicking; still, people flocked to have their pictures taken with them. To help draw the tourists, there were Easter egg hunts using giant ostrich eggs.

In St. Augustine, two men built a trolley line from downtown St. Augustine to the beaches. Along the route, there were a number of alligators, and the men placed them in an abandoned house while they worked.

The men found that the tourists were willing to pay to see the alligators. In 1893, the Alligator Farm opened and has been successful ever since.

In the 1920s, the Ostrich Farm fell on hard times and merged with the Alligator Farm in the 1920s. The Alligator Farm still draws about 200,000 visitors a year, but without the ostriches.

He built eight hotels, including the magnificent Tampa Bay Hotel, a Moorish palace that catered to the very wealthy. When he opened the hotel, he invited Flagler, who wired back, "Where is Tampa Bay?" Plant is supposed to have responded, "Just follow the crowds." The hotel was always unprofitable and, in 1933, became part of the University of Tampa. He built a second resort hotel, the Belleair, in Clearwater. It featured the state's first major golf course and train tracks that allowed the wealthy to bring their private rail cars nearly to the front door.

As historian Tracy Revels found, there was a difference between Flagler and Plant. Flagler developed towns out of the wilderness in Palm Beach, Miami and other spots along his railroad. Plant built his hotels in small towns already established.

Plant did have one idea that had a lasting legacy in the travel industry. He created the inclusive vacation—transportation, hotel and food included in one set price.

While Flagler and Plant are known for their hotels and the tourists they brought, often overlooked are the vast tracts of land they accumulated. Plant and Flagler became the state's largest landowners, controlling hundreds of thousands of acres.

The third railroad baron was the less-well-known William Chipley, whose railroad stretched across the panhandle. His legacy was not in developing resorts but building industries, from lumber to farming to naval stores.

Fishermen and hunters also discovered the state, which seemed to be stocked with an endless supply of wildlife to shoot and catch. Former president Theodore Roosevelt made headlines when he hooked a giant tarpon.

The influx led one writer to observe in 1882, "Florida is rapidly becoming a northern colony."

15

THE EVERGLADES

One of the constant themes in Florida history has been the desire to change the Everglades.

As early as the 1840s, there was talk of draining the Everglades. In 1848, a St. Augustine attorney named Buckingham Smith was hired to study the idea of draining the Everglades. Predictably, Smith's report favored draining—a stand that remained popular for a century.

In 1850, Congress passed the Swamp Land Act of 1850, which was aimed at developing the Everglades. Some twenty million acres in the Everglades was transferred to the state with the idea that the state could turn it over to private companies for development. The Third Seminole War and the presence of the Seminoles in the Everglades put a damper on talk of draining the massive swamp. The Civil War came soon after the Third Seminole War, and the state's precarious financial situation in the 1870s prevented any progress on drainage.

In the 1880s, the state was unable to pay off $1 million in railroad bonds. The desire to pay off the bonds and drain the Everglades came together in a scheme that led to disaster.

Wealthy Philadelphia businessman Hamilton Disston gave the state $1 million to pay off the railroad bonds and received four million acres of land that ranged from damp to underwater. Disston thought he could drain the giant swamp and develop the land. He began digging in 1882, in the upper Kissimmee Valley that flows into Lake Okeechobee, installing a network of canals to drain the water. His work aided in the

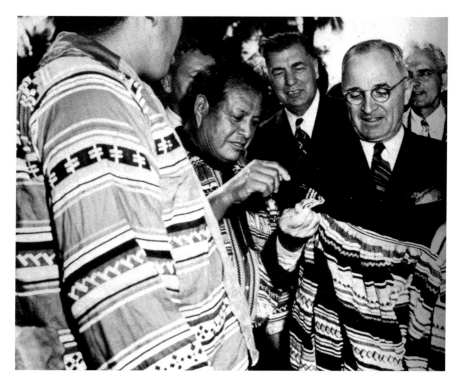

When President Truman dedicated the Everglades National Park in 1947, he met with Seminole Indians. *Florida Archives Photographic Collection.*

development and growth of Kissimmee, St. Cloud, Gulfport, Tarpon Springs and St. Petersburg. It also attracted the railroad kings Henry Plant and Henry Flagler.

Disston was being fooled; the state was undergoing a dry spell, and his plan only seemed to be working. When the rain levels returned to normal, the land he had drained was once again underwater. In fact, the heavy rains brought new flooding, and in the end, the Everglades remained as wet as they had been when Disston arrived.

He created Disston City—which became Gulfport—and his efforts opened parts of Florida to others. He also started the Florida sugar industry, forming the Florida Sugar Manufacturing Company in Clewiston.

Much of his fortune was lost in Florida and debts were piling up. His death was as controversial as his plan to drain the Everglades. Although he was nearly broke, he did have a million-dollar insurance policy—the second largest in the United States. Many believe that he shot himself in his bathtub

THE SUGAR INDUSTRY

Like many things in Florida, the sugar industry traces its roots to the early Spanish explorers. Pedro Menéndez de Ávila brought sugarcane to St. Augustine soon after his arrival in 1565; however, it was not until the British period in 1767 that sugar production began in New Smyrna.

The efforts to get a sugar industry going were interrupted by the American Revolution and then failed because the state's climate was not good for sugar.

It was not until around 1920 that the industry finally got going around Lake Okeechobee, helped by several major developments. New varieties of sugarcane were developed that could thrive in Florida. Second, drainage of the Everglades led to better growing conditions, and third, the federal government began to help the industry with the Sugar Act of 1934.

The sugar industry produced 175,000 tons of raw sugar on about fifty thousand acres in 1960, when an event just ninety miles from Florida gave the industry a major boost. Fidel Castro came to power at the end of 1959, and the United States stopped the importation of sugar from Cuba—the main United States supplier. Soon, the number of mills within the state jumped to eleven, and production more than tripled. By 2000, production passed two million tons a year, about half the domestic sugar output.

Harvesting the sugarcane is tough work. In the early days, it involved standing in the wet soil and using sharp knives to cut the cane. Today, the cane is burned off, though it still requires laborers working under difficult conditions.

In the early 1900s, the promise of work in the sugar industry drew African Americans, but increasingly, they turned to other jobs. The growers began to import foreign workers. In 1943, President Franklin Roosevelt created the guest worker program, which brought workers in from Jamaica, the Bahamas and other Caribbean islands. The program meant that a worker who does not perform up to the grower's expectations could be deported.

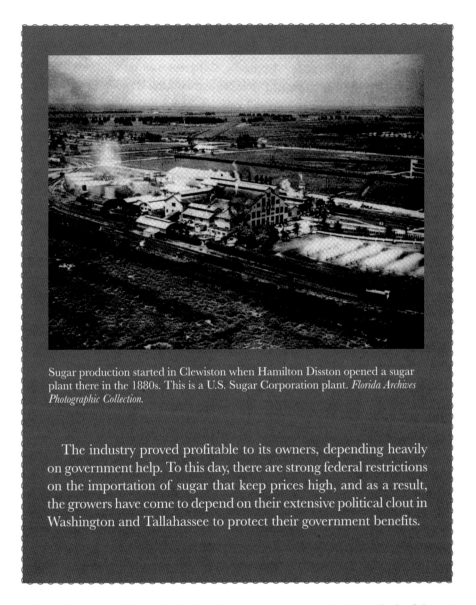

Sugar production started in Clewiston when Hamilton Disston opened a sugar plant there in the 1880s. This is a U.S. Sugar Corporation plant. *Florida Archives Photographic Collection.*

The industry proved profitable to its owners, depending heavily on government help. To this day, there are strong federal restrictions on the importation of sugar that keep prices high, and as a result, the growers have come to depend on their extensive political clout in Washington and Tallahassee to protect their government benefits.

with a shotgun, although the local newspapers reported he died of heart disease at the age of fifty-one. Creditors moved in and foreclosed on his Florida property.

The drainage movement did not die with Disston. In the early 1900s, Governor Napoleon Broward pushed yet another plan to drain the Everglades. Broward personally launched the dredging effort on the New River near Fort Lauderdale with plans to turn the dry land over to settlers.

He had been elected on a platform of draining the Everglades and creating what he called the "Empire of the Everglades."

Broward hoped to build drainage canals connecting Lake Okeechobee with the Atlantic Ocean on the east and the Gulf of Mexico on the west.

In 1913, the legislature gave local governments the right to drain land as they saw fit, without any control from the state. Local governments responded with enthusiasm, and soon there were fifty-two drainage districts.

The 1920s land boom accelerated the demand for land as hundreds of thousands of people moved into Florida, primarily South Florida near Lake Okeechobee. Even though the U.S. Army Corps of Engineers began building larger canals to control the waters of the Everglades, the water levels continued to rise.

Everywhere, the Everglades were being threatened. The lumber was being removed for construction projects while the alligators, birds and fish were hunted nearly to the point of extinction. The beautiful birds were prized for the plumes that adorned women's hats in the late nineteenth and early twentieth century.

A 1926 hurricane broke the Lake Okeechobee levees and hundreds of people drowned—many new arrivals who had recently purchased the land where they would die. Two years later, a second hurricane claimed nearly 2,500 lives when the lake again overflowed.

While an attempt to control the flow of water into the Everglades with the construction of the Herbert Hoover Dike was deemed a success, its construction was followed by a severe drought and wildfires in 1939.

Floridians were slow to realize that Florida's ecosystem was tied to the Everglades—as the Everglades went, so did Florida. As the canals were deepened and widened, salt water replaced fresh water and began seeping into South Florida's water supply.

It is frightening to think what might have happened to the water supply if it had not been for Marjory Stoneman Douglas and her fellow crusaders. In the 1940s, she began studying the Everglades for a book, *Everglades: River of Grass*.

She wrote, "What had been a river of grass and sweet water that had given meaning and life and uniqueness to this enormous geography through centuries in which man had no place here was made, in one chaotic gesture of greed and ignorance and folly, a river of fire."

As early as the 1920s, there were attempts to have all or part of the Everglades become a park and protected. Congress authorized a park in 1934, but not the money to pay for it, and during the Great Depression, private money was difficult to raise.

In 1947, President Harry S. Truman dedicated the Everglades National Park. The park suffered because existing canals were cutting off its water supply. An attempt to place an international airport in the Everglades drew widespread opposition, and the plan was killed.

Slowly—too slowly many believe—the Corps of Engineers turned from developing land around the park to protecting it.

Draining the Everglades is not the only scheme that has threatened Florida's environment. King Philip II of Spain first proposed a canal across Florida in 1567, and the idea stayed alive for four hundred years.

As historians David Tegeder and Steve Noll found, the canal was kept alive for a number of reasons. For the Spanish, it meant a shorter and safer route from its Latin American colonies to Spain. The ships could avoid the pirates lurking along the coast, waiting for treasure to sail up the Gulf Stream, or the deadly hurricanes that sent scores of ships to the bottom.

The storms and the pirates continued into the 1800s, and Secretary of War John C. Calhoun was the first American government official to propose a canal, even though Florida still belonged to Spain.

The plan was to follow the St. Johns River to Palatka and then utilize the Ocklawaha River and the Withlacoochee River to the Gulf of Mexico.

The Great Depression gave the canal new life as supporters saw it as a way to create thousands of jobs rather than the primary reason—shipping goods more quickly. In 1935, as opponents began to claim that the canal would damage the aquifer, President Roosevelt gave some money, but the federal grant was not renewed.

World War II gave it new life as supporters claimed that building the canal would help the war effort by making shipping faster and safer. Money was appropriated, but construction never actually began.

President John Kennedy gave $1 million to the project, but it was Lyndon Johnson who gave the canal the greatest support. He pushed the button that set off a symbolic blast to start construction, which was to be completed in 1971.

Some digging took place amid growing opposition. In 1971, President Richard Nixon stopped construction. It languished another two decades before it was officially cancelled.

16

PRESIDENTS AND FLORIDA

For the early presidents of the United States, Florida was a problem—a thorn in their side to be dealt with.

For George Washington, the problems began when he was commander of American forces during the American Revolution. Florida was a British colony and remained loyal to King George. That meant that Florida was a haven for the Loyalists in the colonies and for escaped slaves.

After the American Revolution, Florida returned to Spanish control, and both Spain and the United States claimed parts of present-day Alabama and Mississippi. Washington sent a negotiator to work out a boundary with Spain.

Jefferson tried to acquire Florida, even claiming that he had purchased West Florida as part of the Louisiana Purchase. His claim was ignored. Even after he left the White House, he continued to push for the acquisition of Florida.

Florida became what one historian called the Wild West of the southeast with Indian raids into the United States, pirates using Florida ports, criminals hiding out and slaves using it as a sanctuary.

Spain was unable to defend its territory and could not do anything to stop the troubles. Two brothers made attempts to seize West Florida, and in 1810, they captured the Spanish fort at Baton Rouge. President James Madison responded by seizing West Florida. During the War of 1812, American troops captured the Spanish city of Mobile.

President James Madison sent a secret agent named George Mathews to Georgia to organize a revolution to take the rest of Florida. The expedition failed for a number of reasons, and Madison did not acquire Florida.

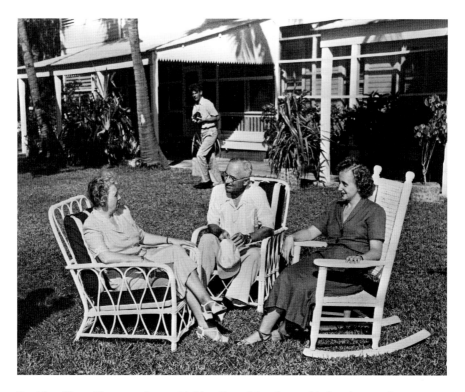

President Harry Truman relaxes with his wife and daughter at his favorite vacation spot, Key West. Truman spent eight months of his eight-year presidency in Key West. *Florida Archives Photographic Collection.*

James Monroe came to the White House next, and there was no president who was more interested in Florida. For two decades, he tried to acquire Florida, first as a diplomat and then as president. He sent Andrew Jackson to stop the raids into the United States, and Jackson thought he was being sent to take Florida. Monroe disavowed the expedition when other nations protested.

In 1819, Monroe opened negotiations to acquire Florida and, two years later, finally acquired it.

John Tyler came to the presidency when William Henry Harrison died shortly after his inauguration. Tyler was a supporter of statehood for Florida—primarily because he was a supporter of slavery and wanted another slave state in the Union. On his last day as president, he signed the legislation admitting Florida as a state.

Florida helped Zachary Taylor on his way to the White House. He first made his reputation fighting the Seminole Indians in Florida, which led him to command American troops in the Mexican-American War and then on to the White House.

Ulysses S. Grant came to Florida in 1880 looking for a political comeback. He had served two terms and left the White House in 1877. Grant wanted another term and was on a tour seeking publicity and delegates. In Florida, he went to Sanford to dedicate the railroad being built from Sanford to Tampa. Grant failed to win the nomination, although the Florida delegation remained with him until the end.

President James A. Garfield received a most unusual honor in Florida—having what became a ghost town named for him. Garfield was mortally wounded four months into his term. A group of former slaves honored him by naming their Central Florida town after him. The village of Garfield had a post office, a train depot and a store. But a freeze in the 1880s wiped out the crops, and the town was abandoned. Everyone was gone by the 1890 census.

Chester A. Arthur became president when Garfield died and became the first sitting president to visit Florida. In 1883, he took a government mail train to Jacksonville, then a steamboat up the St. Johns River to Sanford and a train to Kissimmee, where he went fishing at the site of what became Disney World sixty years later.

Arthur's successor, Grover Cleveland, also came to Florida, enjoying the warm weather.

Just as Zachary Taylor had been sent on his way to the White House by events in Florida, Teddy Roosevelt also found his start to the presidency in Florida.

Roosevelt and his Rough Riders assembled in Tampa for a trip by boat to Cuba. The number of soldiers far outnumbered the boats to get them to Cuba. Roosevelt was able to force his way onto one of the ships—ignoring the fact that he was not supposed to board—and made his fame at the Battle of San Juan Hill.

His most significant contribution in Florida was wildlife preservation. Many of Florida's most beautiful birds were hunted by the thousands for their beautiful plumes, which were used in women's hats. Roosevelt signed an executive order making Pelican Island the first federal bird reservation. He went on to establish fifty-four more reservations, including ten in Florida. Roosevelt also created the Ocala National Forest in 1908, the oldest national forest east of the Mississippi. He also created Choctawhatchee National Forest in the Florida Panhandle the same year.

Warren G. Harding came to Florida to work, something that usually gave way to drinking, golf or playing cards. He came in early 1921, after being elected president, to work on his cabinet and inaugural address. While on

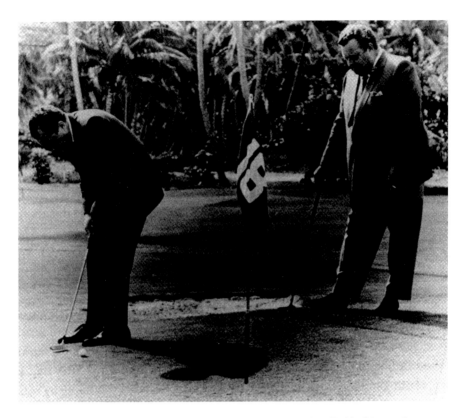

Before his election in 1968, Richard Nixon putted with entertainer Jackie Gleason in Miami. Gleason moved his popular television program to Miami Beach, bringing the area tremendous publicity in the days before *Miami Vice*. *Florida Archives Photographic Collection.*

a friend's yacht, he became stuck on a sandbar in the Indian River near Titusville and could not leave until the tide rose the next day. He also helped to promote the new resort of Miami Beach. Carl Fisher, one of the world's greatest promoters, came up with his best idea ever: Fisher used an elephant as Harding's caddy.

Harding's successor, Calvin Coolidge, loved Florida and was a frequent visitor. He visited the "Senator," a giant tree outside Orlando and took part in the dedication of the Bok Tower in Lake Wales.

Like Coolidge, Herbert Hoover was a frequent visitor to Florida. Fishing and camping were his primary attractions. For years, he held the record for the largest bonefish caught in Florida, and he went camping with Henry Ford, Harvey Firestone and Thomas Edison. When he went to Miami, he stayed at the mansion of J.C. Penney.

Hoover was the first Republican presidential candidate to carry Florida since Reconstruction, which was more of a vote against his Catholic, pro-alcohol opponent, Al Smith. When the Great Depression struck, Hoover's popularity with Floridians declined, and he lost Florida in 1932.

Harry Truman spent more time in Florida than any other president. Of the nearly eight years he was in the White House, he spent a total of eight months in Florida. While he liked the warm weather, Truman had little money, and his vacations in Florida were free. Navy ships or the presidential train took him to Florida, and he stayed at the navy base. He stayed there so often that the building where he stayed is still known as the "Little White House."

John Kennedy's family purchased a home in Palm Beach in the 1930s, and he underwent his military training in Florida. After the war, he came to Palm Beach to recover from frequent back surgery. While recovering from one surgery, he wrote the Pulitzer Prize–winning *Profiles in Courage* and later worked on his acclaimed inaugural address at Palm Beach.

Richard Nixon was the last president to spend extended amounts of time in Florida. Shortly after he was elected president, he bought a home in Key Biscayne and became a frequent visitor. He was at the Key Biscayne White House when he learned that there had been a break in at the Watergate complex—an event that brought down his presidency.

Today, presidents spend very little time in Florida. They come often for fundraisers and to speak to conventions, spending only a few hours before they are back on Air Force One and out of Florida.

Florida first voted in the 1848 election, three years after becoming a state. Predictably, the state voted for Zachary Taylor, a Whig, who had directed troops in Florida.

The state swung to the Democratic column four years later and, except for a handful of elections, stayed there for the next century.

The Republican Party nominated its first presidential candidate in 1856—John C. Frémont; however, Floridians could not vote for him. In that election, and four years later when the Republicans nominated Abraham Lincoln, state officials refused to put them on the ballot. Instead, on the eve of the Civil War, the presidential ballot included three Democrats, with John C. Breckinridge winning the state.

Twice, Florida has played the major role in the determining the president of the United States; otherwise, since 1928, the state voted with the winner in twenty elections.

The first significant election came during Reconstruction. The Republicans carried the state—thanks to voting limitations put on former Confederates.

In the 1876 election, all the former Confederates could vote for the Democratic candidate while the Ku Klux Klan discouraged African American voters from casting ballots for the Republicans. This set up confusing results in the contest between Democrat Samuel J. Tilden and Republican Rutherford B. Hayes. It was impossible to tell for certain who had carried the state.

Tilden held a comfortable margin in the popular national vote and won 184 electoral votes, just one short of the number needed for election. The results in Florida, Louisiana and North Carolina were so confused that the Republicans saw a chance to win.

Both political parties sent operatives into Florida and claimed victory. In the end, Florida went with the Republican candidate as part of a political deal that brought an end to Reconstruction and guaranteed that Democrats would once again control state politics.

The second significant election came in 2000, when the result was decided by Florida and the U.S. Supreme Court. The Democratic candidate, Al Gore, led in the popular vote nationwide, and he was within a handful of electoral votes needed for victory. The Republican nominee, George W. Bush, needed Florida to win, but the popular vote was in dispute. No one can say who really carried the state—the official margin showed Bush leading by about five hundred votes out of six million cast.

But thousands of votes were in dispute, and both sides claimed victory. The two campaigns sent political operatives and attorneys into the state to attempt to influence the outcome. Recounts were begun, and both sides began filing legal briefs. Finally, the U.S. Supreme Court put an end to the recounts and awarded the state to Bush in the case *Bush v. Gore*.

From 1880 to 1928, Florida voted for the Democratic candidate in every election. Usually the margins were overwhelming, and usually Florida was voting for the loser. For example, in 1900, William McKinley won the presidency without any help from Florida, where he carried just 18 percent of the vote.

In 1928, Florida voted for the Republican candidate, Herbert Hoover, not so much because the voters support Hoover as because they voted against his opponent, New York governor Al Smith. First, Smith was a Catholic, and Protestant preachers took to their pulpits to warn their congregations of the evils of a vote for Smith. He was also for the repeal of Prohibition, and conservative Florida would not support that. They heard his heavy New York City accent on their radios and cast their ballots for Hoover.

Hoover's popularity came crashing down along with the stock market in 1929. In 1928, Hoover received 57 percent of the vote in Florida, but in 1932, he received just 25 percent. Florida and the nation went with Franklin Roosevelt.

Florida stuck with Roosevelt through four elections and with Truman for one before voting for Dwight D. Eisenhower in two elections. Richard Nixon won the state in 1960, 1968 and 1972, with Democrat Lyndon Johnson carrying the state by a narrow margin in 1964.

The southern appeal of Jimmy Carter brought Florida back to the Democrats in 1976—Carter was the first southerner to win the White House since Woodrow Wilson. Ronald Reagan had no trouble winning two elections for the Republicans, and George H.W. Bush won in 1988.

Bush also carried Florida in 1992 as the nation elected Bill Clinton. In the five elections since 1996, Florida has gone with the winner.

Florida is the largest state in the nation to never have had a presidential or vice presidential candidate or even a nominee by a major political party. Florida has become a key state politically—no Republican since Calvin Coolidge has won the White House without carrying Florida—but its politicians are overlooked when it comes to being national candidates.

Three former governors—Claude Kirk, Reubin Askew and Bob Graham—sought the presidency, but their campaigns never gained traction.

17

BOURBON FLORIDA

The end of Reconstruction brought the beginning of what became known as the Bourbon era. It lasted during the last quarter of the nineteenth century and was dominated by conservative Democrats. The Bourbons had begun during Reconstruction to battle the Republicans.

The Bourbons took control of Florida in the 1868 election and adopted a pro-business, anti-tax, pro-development, anti-education and increasingly anti–African American platform. Keeping taxes low meant funding schools and social programs meagerly, and the legislature even considered closing down the public schools from time to time.

Keeping taxes low and giving sweeping benefits to businesses meant the state made promises it could not keep. Florida borrowed money and could not pay it back. The state owed $1 million and, in desperation, agreed to sell four million acres for twenty-five cents an acre to Philadelphia businessman Hamilton Disston.

Disston's plan ended in disaster, but the money helped the state launch a massive railroad building program. When Bloxham took office, the state had 556 miles of track, and in ten years, the mileage had increased 500 percent and another one thousand miles were added by 1900.

For every mile of track, the railroads were given land—millions of acres—by the state, and they began selling the land to settlers. And with each mile the railroads gained more influence in state government. The railroads shipped the state's vegetables and oranges and could charge whatever they

TIMELINE 1887-1918

1887: Eatonville, the oldest surviving incorporated black community in the United States, is established.

1894–95: Freezes destroy citrus crops in North and Central Florida, pushing the citrus industry south.

1898: Florida becomes the launching ground for the Spanish-American War with bases at Tampa, Miami, Lakeland and Jacksonville.

1900: Greek immigrants arrive and settle in Tarpon Springs.

1901: Fire destroys downtown Jacksonville.

1905: Construction begins on Henry Flagler's Overseas Railroad to Key West.

1914: The first regularly scheduled commercial airline flight takes place between St. Petersburg and Tampa.

1917: Florida is the site of training and shipbuilding during World War I.

wanted. The saying, "Charge anything the traffic will bear," referred to the railroads' ability not only to charge what they wanted but also to change the prices at any time.

The farmers were at the mercy of the railroads, and by the 1880s, they were in revolt. They joined the Populist movement, which demanded regulation of the railroads. Governor Wilkinson Call created a railroad commission to regulate the railroads. The reality was that the commission had no enforcement powers, and the railroads simply ignored the rules.

Farmers also flocked to join the Patrons of Husbandry, known as the Grange, which held meetings to discuss common problems, and eventually turned to politics to have more influence. The Grange was successful in electing members to the legislature.

The railroad boom opened all of Florida to development and settlement, but it also contributed to a financial panic in 1893, which drove many farmers and citrus growers into bankruptcy and even forced some smaller railroads into bankruptcy.

VOTING FOR WOMEN

In 1912, the Florida Equal Franchise League was created to campaign for the vote for women. The league had its headquarters in Jacksonville. The same year, a group of women tried to vote in Florida during a municipal election in Orlando but were turned away.

The league had between seven and eight hundred members. One member, seventy-three-year-old Mary Nolan of Jacksonville, went to Washington to picket the White House and spent six days in jail.

The Florida legislature considered approving a constitutional amendment to give women the right to vote, but the bill died with little debate. State representative John M. Gornto of Lafayette County told the legislature that giving women the right to vote would "bring on marital unhappiness, divorces, and a disruptive domestic condition."

The amendment was approved by the required number of states, but even as it became the law of the land, Florida did not approve it. In 1969, in a meaningless vote, Florida passed the amendment giving women the right to vote.

18

THE SPANISH-AMERICAN WAR

The Cuban Revolution of 1868 led thousands of Cubans to seek safety in the United States. Most settled in Key West, Tampa or New York. The Cuban turmoil caused cigar manufacturers to flee and set up factories in the United States.

Vicente Martínez Ybor purchased forty acres of land near downtown Tampa in 1885, founding Ybor City, home to cigar factories and the cigar workers.

The factories became centers for the revolutionary movement, which continued to simmer even after the 1868 revolution failed. The cigar workers contributed part of their salaries to fund the work of revolutionary leader José Martí. During a visit to Tampa there was an attempt to poison Martí by Spanish agents.

This did not mean that the majority of Floridians supported going to war with Spain over Cuba. As war fever in the rest of the United States increased, Floridians held back. There were reasons for the reluctance. Florida is the closest state to Cuba, and Floridians did not know that Spain had become a third-rate power incapable of launching an attack on their state. The federal government posted military units along the coastal areas to calm their fears.

The biggest concern was economic; if the United States won the war—a certainty—the United States might acquire Cuba as a territory. Cuba's economy mirrored that of Florida, with oranges, tobacco, cigars and even the beginnings of a tourist industry. The Teller Amendment was passed to ease those concerns; it stipulated that the United States would not acquire Cuba as a territory.

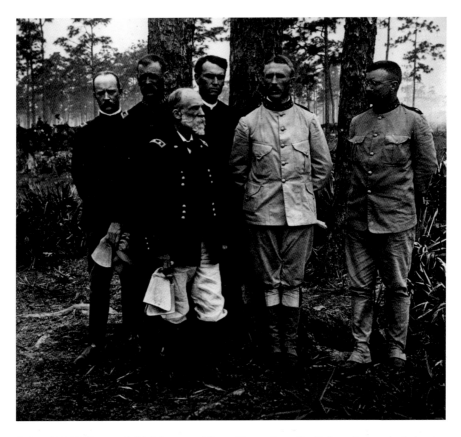

Colonel Teddy Roosevelt (right) poses while waiting to leave for Cuba, where a single battle propelled him into the White House. *Library of Congress.*

On February 15, 1898, the USS *Maine* exploded in Havana Harbor, killing two out of three crewmen and fanning war fever. American newspaper publishers, led by William Randolph Hearst and Joseph Pulitzer, called for war and shouted the slogan "Remember the *Maine*, to Hell with Spain!" President William McKinley yielded to the pressure for war.

While Florida had resisted the war, once war was declared, Florida was a prime beneficiary. The War Department decided that Tampa would be the military headquarters for the war—it was close to Cuba but safe from a possible Spanish attack. Miami had a good port, but the village was just two years old and lacked facilities.

Nearly twenty-five thousand troops jammed Tampa, overwhelming the small town. The number included Lieutenant Colonel Theodore Roosevelt

THE CUBAN REVOLUTIONS

For nearly five hundred years, people have emigrated from Cuba to the United States. During the Spanish era, Florida and Louisiana were under the jurisdiction of Cuba.

Even before the arrival of Ponce de León in 1513, there were indications that there had been earlier trade between Cuba and the Indians in Florida. During the Spanish period, thousands of settlers migrated from Cuba to Florida, Louisiana and Texas.

A ten-year revolution broke out in Cuba in 1868, as the Cubans sought their independence from Spain. It was the first of three revolutions to take place over the next thirty years, and each would send thousands of Cubans to the United States.

The first wave of immigrants came in 1870 and settled in New York, New Orleans and Key West. Although New York drew the largest number of the early settlers, Key West and later Tampa began to attract more and more Cubans.

In the last third of the nineteenth century, Key West came to depend on Cuban tobacco production to keep its economy alive. Tampa also drew Cuban tobacco workers, primarily cigar makers. The town grew from 720 residents in 1880 to over 5,000 in 1890.

As the violence in Cuba increased, more of the Cuban cigar makers moved their operations to the safety of Florida. The section of Tampa occupied by the new Cubans and the cigar factories became known as Ybor City. Key West and Tampa became centers for supporting and financing the Cuban Revolution. Revolutionary leader José Martí came to Florida seeking help to finance the revolution.

After the Spanish-American War, some Cubans returned to their homeland, but many stayed in the United States.

During the first half of the twentieth century there were new waves of Cuban immigrants. Some immigrants came during political upheavals while others arrived during economic hard times in the island.

By 1958, there were 125,000 Cuban-Americans living in the United States.

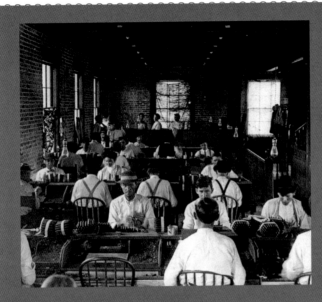

Cuban immigrants work at a cigar factory in Ybor City. *Florida Archives Photographic Collection.*

In 1959, Fidel Castro came into power and set off a massive exodus to the United States. Over two decades, hundreds of thousands of Cubans came to the United States.

The first group to arrive came immediately after Castro came to power. Most of the early arrivals were from the upper and middle classes, including friends and associates of the ousted dictator Fulgencio Batista. Some Cuban parents stayed in Cuba, but sent their children to the United States to live with relatives, stay in foster homes or even orphanages. The city of Miami and the state of Florida were overwhelmed by the influx and could not cope with the demands. The federal government was forced to step in, passing the Cuban Adjustment Act in 1966 to provide aid to the immigrants. There were attempts to disperse the Cubans around the country, but most settled in Miami.

In the 1980s, an estimated 125,000 more Cubans came, part of what were known as the Mariel boatlift. By 2010, there were 1.2 million Cuban-Americans living in Florida. The second-largest concentration was in California, where there were 88,000.

and his Rough Riders, who rode to fame at San Juan Hill. The army set up its headquarters in Henry Plant's Tampa Bay Hotel. The city was so full that troops were stationed as far away as Lakeland.

At every turn, Henry Plant made money from the war. He had lobbied hard to have the headquarters brought to Tampa, sending an aide to meet with officials of the McKinley administration. The results could be seen everywhere; the trains were backed up as far north as Ocala, thousands of freight cars waiting to unload their supplies. For the first time, all 511 rooms at Plant's Tampa Bay Hotel were filled, and there was a long waiting list.

Roosevelt and his wife, Edith, stayed at the Tampa Bay Hotel, as did artist Frederick Remington, writer Stephen Crane and Clara Barton, who headed a Red Cross unit. There were far more soldiers than were needed, and many realized they would be left behind. The rush to board the ships injured scores of soldiers, as thousands missed out on their moment of glory.

On June 14, 1898, sixteen thousand troops on thirty-five ships sailed for Cuba as the band played "Hot Time in the Old Town Tonight."

Plant's steamship, the SS *Olivette*, was used to transport men and supplies to the army.

In Miami, the soldiers stationed there complained of the conditions. One soldier wrote to his parents, "If I owned both Miami and Hell, I'd sell Miami and go to live in Hell." As the threat of a Spanish invasion faded, the camps in Miami and Fernandina were shut down.

While 260 Americans died in battle in Cuba, the real threat was from disease, primarily yellow fever—which killed ten times as many soldiers as combat.

As with all wars the United States has fought, Florida came out a winner. Not only were millions of dollars poured into the state, the federal government had to build infrastructure to support its military effort. Most importantly, the majority of those who came to Florida were seeing it for the first time, and many liked what they saw. When the war was over, they stayed in Florida—or came back—touching off a building boom that would continue into the 1920s.

19

SPORTS IN FLORIDA

Three thousand years ago, the Apalachee Indians played the first sport in Florida. One village would meet another village on an open field for a game that vaguely resembled soccer or kickball. As many as one hundred players participated on each team, using a ball about the size of a modern golf ball covered with leather. The players kicked the ball toward a goal post, which was a pole with a stuffed eagle on top.

Ever since, sports have played an important role in Florida.

When the tourists began arriving in the late 1800s, they had money to spend and looked for things to do. Ostrich racing became an attraction. The birds were brought into the United States in the 1880s, and by 1890, there was an ostrich track in Jacksonville. Others opened in St. Augustine and St. Petersburg.

Golf came to Florida in 1886 when J. Hamilton Gillespie laid out two greens and a fairway on what is now Main Street in downtown Sarasota. It was a small start—Gillespie was usually the only one using his "course," but his main contribution was convincing Henry Plant that golf courses would be good for business.

The following year, Plant opened a golf course with six holes in nearby St. Petersburg, following Gillespie's design, and the state's first country club, Belleair Country Club, was born. Gillespie also designed courses in Winter Park, Tampa and Havana, Cuba.

Plant's friendly competitor Henry Flagler also saw the value of golf, but his early hotels—such as the one in St. Augustine—had little room for a golf course. It was not until 1897 that Flagler build the first regulation, eighteen-hole course at the Breakers in Palm Beach.

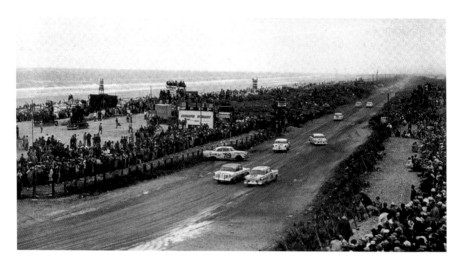

Daytona Beach drew thousands for racing on the beach in 1956. Three years later, what is now Daytona International Speedway opened. *Florida Archives Photographic Collection.*

The boom years of the 1920s saw an explosion of courses. The Mission Inn Golf and Tennis Resort near Orlando opened in 1926, and the Naples Beach Hotel and Golf Club began in what became downtown Naples.

Legendary course designer Donald Ross planned courses in St. Augustine, Delray, Clearwater and Fort Myers.

Robert Trent Jones created the Turnberry Isle Resort & Club, and Herbert Bertram Strong created what is considered the state's most famous course, Ponte Vedra Inn & Club. Strong set out to design a difficult course along Florida's coast near Jacksonville.

Florida became the home to major tournaments, including the Players Championship at Ponte Vedra. Today, Florida has more than one thousand golf courses.

Boxing also became popular in Florida. In 1894, James J. Corbett defeated Charley Mitchell for the heavyweight boxing championship in Jacksonville. Corbett collected $20,000 for knocking out Mitchell in the third round, even though Corbett complained that referee "Honest John" Kelly was not counting fast enough. In one of boxing's biggest fights, Jack Sharkey defeated W.L. Young at Miami Beach in 1929 before forty thousand fans, including gangster Al Capone. In one of boxing's greatest upsets, Muhammad Ali became heavyweight champion when he defeated the overwhelming favorite Sonny Liston in 1964 at Miami Beach.

BASEBALL

Throughout the first half century of Major League Baseball, spring training was haphazard. Teams chose cities such as Cairo, Illinois; Hot Springs, Arkansas; and Valdosta, Georgia. Some cash-starved teams stayed home and merely worked out for a few days before the season began.

In 1889, the Philadelphia Phillies spent two weeks training in Jacksonville but played elsewhere before returning to Florida permanently.

In 1913, Branch Rickey, the manager of the St. Louis Browns, took his team to St. Petersburg for training. More than four decades later, Rickey integrated Major League Baseball when he signed Jackie Robinson to play for the Brooklyn Dodgers. The Chicago Cubs set up camp in neighboring Tampa.

The Boston Red Sox and the New York Yankees came after World War II, although the Yankees moved several times before settling in Tampa.

Babe Ruth hit one of the longest home runs in baseball—579 yards—in Tampa, but he claimed that an alligator lived in a lake along the outfield and refused to go out there.

In 1929, the Detroit Tigers began playing in Arizona, and other teams followed. Eventually, Major League Baseball split with half the teams in Florida and the other half in Arizona.

Baseball's spring training came to Florida in 1901 and became a major tourist attraction.

The early builders of automobiles had little money but a desperate need to test their cars. They needed a wide, flat, empty area—and it needed to be free. They chose a twenty-three-mile stretch of packed sand that was five hundred feet wide at low tide, extending north from Daytona Beach.

Henry Flagler owned the magnificent hotel at Ormond Beach, and he drew his wealthy friends, including oil magnet John D. Rockefeller, who visited the beach and watched the cars being tested. There was always the chance that one of them would invest in the cars.

Beginning in 1903, land speed records were set at Ormond Beach. Two of those carmakers who came to Ormond became world famous: Henry Ford—who was so broke he had to sleep in his car—and Ransom Olds, builder of the Oldsmobile. Soon, world speed records were being set at Daytona. In 1903, Olds recorded a speed of 68 miles per hour. A year later, millionaire William K. Vanderbilt reached 92 miles per hour in his Mercedes. By 1905, speeds passed 100 miles per hour. The fastest speed was recorded by Malcolm Campbell, who reached 276 miles per hour in 1935.

In 1935, William France Sr. moved to Daytona Beach to look for work. Like millions of others, he had been hurt by the Great Depression. He had a love of cars and knew of the area's racing history. In 1936, he entered a race and finished fifth. Within three years, he was running the races and came up with the idea that people would watch races involving regular cars—or stock cars—not just specially designed race cars.

There were already races, but the business was loaded with crooks who often disappeared with the prize money. In 1948, France organized NASCAR, the National Association for Stock Car Auto Racing. His organization brought order to the chaos of racing and made sure rules were followed. Using a napkin from the hotel where the NASCAR organizers were meeting, France and others mapped out a point system.

NASCAR grew slowly and eventually became one of the most popular sports in terms of television ratings, and it is still controlled by the France family.

The 1920s also saw the birth of greyhound racing in Florida. In 1919, O.P. Smith invented the electric rabbit and a circular track for greyhound racing at Hialeah in 1922, replacing the live jackrabbits that were sometimes killed while fans watched. The St. Petersburg Kennel Club opened in 1925, and soon there were greyhound tracks throughout the state.

By the 1840s, there were three horseracing tracks, all in the Florida Panhandle. At the now defunct town of St. Joseph's, the five-day racing season brought large crowds and cash prizes. There was even a Jockey Club Ball. During the boom of the 1920s, Tampa Downs and Hialeah Racetrack opened, and Gulfstream came in 1936.

Despite all these sports, for most of its history, Florida lacked the population to attract a major-league team. The story was the same throughout the South. In fact, the professional football team most Floridians rooted for were the Washington Redskins, and Florida radio stations carried the team's games.

The first attempt at a major-league team ended in disaster. The Miami Seahawks played in the All-American Football Conference in 1946, ran up a $350,000 debt and then folded. Eventually, the team became the Indianapolis Colts. It was another twenty years before Miami got another major team, the Dolphins of the American Football League, a challenger to the National Football League. In 1970, the leagues merged, and Florida had its first NFL team. The team made NFL history in 1972, when it finished a perfect season and won the Super Bowl, a feat no other team has accomplished. The team's coach Don Shula became an NFL legend.

The Tampa Bay Buccaneers joined the NFL in 1976 and became a laughingstock as they lost their first twenty-six games. They won the 2002 Super Bowl under coach Jon Gruden. Jacksonville had long sought an NFL team but was constantly rebuffed until 1995, when it landed the Jacksonville Jaguars.

Professional ice hockey came in 1992 with the Tampa Bay Lightning playing before eleven thousand fans in a tiny arena on the state fairgrounds. A year later, the Florida Panthers began playing in Miami. The Lightning won the Stanley Cup in 2004.

Professional baseball came to Miami in 1993, when the Marlins began playing. St. Petersburg spent thirty years trying to get a Major League Baseball team before landing the Tampa Bay Devil Rays for the 1998 season.

Football was always the leading sport in Florida, and basketball was something of an afterthought. Professional basketball first came to Florida in 1968, when the Minnesota Muskies of the American Basketball Association moved to Miami and became the Floridians. The team was known for erratic and miserable management. At one point, the team played in an old aircraft hangar without air conditioning. To provide ventilation, the hangar doors were opened, which often brought stiff breezes, making shooting difficult. One year, the team rotated its games among Tampa, Jacksonville, St. Petersburg, Miami and West Palm Beach. In one bizarre move, the owner fired the entire team. Unable to find a buyer, or a place to relocate, the team folded in 1972.

Basketball returned in 1988, when the National Basketball Association's Miami Heat began playing. The team was plagued by a miserable performance. In 1995, cruise-line owner Micky Arison purchased the team and began turning it around. The team won the NBA championship in 2006. When the team added LeBron James and Chris Bosh to a roster that already included Dwyane Wade, it appeared a dynasty was being born. The team won championships in 2012 and 2013 but lost in 2014. James returned to the Cleveland Cavaliers, but Bosh and Wade remained.

One year after professional basketball came to Miami, the Orlando Magic premiered. It was the first big-time team for Orlando. The team advanced to the NBA finals only once, in 1995 with Shaquille O'Neal leading the way. The team was swept by the Houston Rockets.

Professional soccer has an uneven history in Florida. During the 1970s and 1980s, the North American Soccer League fielded a number of teams in Florida, including Jacksonville, Tampa, Fort Lauderdale and Miami. But the league fell victim to overexpansion and folded. In 2014, Major League Soccer awarded expansion teams to Orlando and Miami.

Even with the presence of so many professional teams, the state's colleges are still the favorites. As early as the 1890s, Stetson, West Florida Seminary (now FSU) and Florida Agricultural College (now UF) had football teams. Rollins added the sport in 1904 but dropped it in 1949 when the coach quit and the school sold off the uniforms to pay its debts. The first college football game was played in Jacksonville in 1901 between Florida Agricultural College and Stetson University, which Stetson won 6-0.

At the time, Florida Agricultural College was located in Lake City. The University of Florida fielded its first official football team in 1906. In the century it has played football, Florida has won three national championships. The school's basketball team won two national championships. The university is a charter member of the Southeastern Conference.

Florida State University traces the start of its athletic program to 1902, when Florida State College played the first of three seasons. In 1905, the state reorganized its secondary education, changing Florida State to Florida State College for Women, and the football players moved to the University of Florida. Returning World War II veterans created demand for a college education, and in 1947, the school began admitting men and became Florida State University. Football returned to FSU in 1948, and the team faced Stetson University for its first game in more than four decades. The FSU team wore its garnet and gold colors for the first time in the 14-6 loss. The team started in the Dixie Conference with such schools as Stetson, Florida Southern College and the University of Tampa. The team won three conference titles, then became an independent school and finally joined the Atlantic Coast Conference. Florida State has won three national championships in football.

The University of Miami began playing football in 1926, and for most of its history, it was a football doormat. In the 1980s, the school's fortunes changed, and between 1983 and 2001, the Hurricanes won five national championships. For most of its history, it was an independent, and then in 1991, Miami joined the Atlantic Coast Conference.

The University of South Florida and the University of Central Florida are relative newcomers to big-time college football—both are in the American Athletic Conference, the successor to the Big East Conference.

20

THE NEW TOURISTS

Whether it was Sidney Lanier writing poetry about Florida or an advertising executive offering, "When you need it bad, we've got it good," Florida's goal has been to lure visitors to its borders.

Tourism is Florida's largest industry. Other states may depend on factories, but Florida needs the revenue from the tens of millions of tourists who come each year.

Henry Plant and Henry Flagler created the Florida tourism industry with their railroads and hotels, but they primarily sought wealthy visitors. It could be expensive to get to Florida, and there were few moderately priced hotels.

The situation remained that way until around World War I. Then, two things happened to make Florida a popular destination for workingmen and women. First was the popularity of the automobile, particularly Henry Ford's attractively priced Model T. Millions of Americans could afford to drive to Florida. At the same time, a highway system linking Florida with the rest of the world became a reality. It started in 1911 with the Atlantic Highway—which became U.S. 1—from Maine to Miami. The highway reached reaching Miami in 1915. In the 1930s, it was extended to Key West.

The Dixie Highway was first proposed in 1914 to link the Midwest with Florida. At first, it was the work of individuals led by Miami Beach developer Carl Fisher, but then the federal government became involved in financing the roads.

The original road stretched from Chicago to Miami. Additions were made, and the road eventually stretched to Sault Ste. Marie, Michigan.

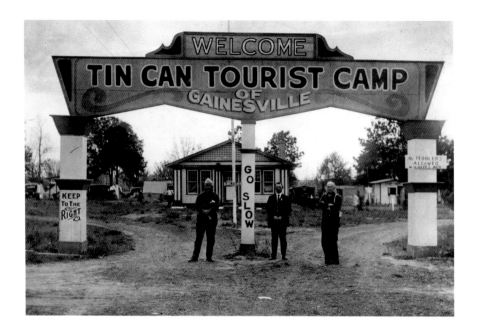

The growing popularity of automobiles and construction of highways in the 1920s brought thousands of tourists who stayed in camps established for the "Tin Can" tourists. This one is near Gainesville. *Florida Archives Photographic Collection.*

In northern factories, stores and small businesses, the idea of vacations for workers spread. Employees could drive to Florida and enjoy the sunshine just like the millionaires. They came by the millions, and many were known as tin-can tourists, who often slept in their cars—which were sometimes converted to homemade recreational vehicles. Their diet consisted largely of beans from tin cans, hence the name. Floridians complained that they came to Florida with a twenty-dollar bill and one shirt and didn't change either.

The tin-can tourists began to establish auto camps in 1919, and they were known to their fellow members by the tin cans they soldered on their radiator cap. There was an official handshake and even a song, "The More We Get Together." The coming of the house trailer in the 1920s meant more tourists, and by the 1940s, there were 300,000 trailers on the road.

In 1926, nearly two million tourists came to Florida. By the 1940s, the number reached three million, even after falling to one million during the Depression.

While the workers often slept in their cars, their bosses wanted luxury. An employee of Harvey Firestone's Akron tire factory might take a short drive to the Dixie Highway and travel south through Kentucky, Tennessee,

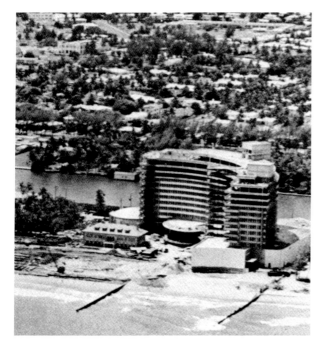

The sprawling Fontainebleau Hotel changed the face of Miami Beach when it opened in 1954. In this photo, it is still under construction, and Harvey Firestone's mansion can be seen in the foreground. The fifteen-bedroom mansion became a construction office and then was demolished. *Florida Archives Photographic Collection.*

Georgia and into Florida. Meanwhile, Firestone could travel in his private railway car to Miami and the huge mansion he built on Miami Beach.

Everywhere there was something to draw tourists. In addition to the weather, the visitors would enjoy baseball's spring training, horseracing, dog racing or a sport imported from Cuba called jai alai. Beginning in 1931, visitors could gamble on which horse, dog or jai alai player would win.

The money brought corruption. There was illegal liquor that flowed during Prohibition, illegal casinos and the beautiful bathing beauties on the beach. One person noted that there were two open saloons within blocks of a Miami police precinct, and casinos often posted signs without worrying that they would be raided. In Nassau and Grand Bahama, huge warehouses were built to house liquor destined for Florida. Fleets of what became known as "Bimini boats" were built just to speed the liquor to Florida.

In an era when gangsters dominated the news, Florida had its share. Al Capone purchased a house on Palm Island between Miami and Miami Beach. Ma Barker and her son, Fred, on the run from the law, were killed by the Federal Bureau of Investigation in Ocklawaha in 1935. Florida's own Ashley Gang seldom made headlines outside of Florida, but its members caused mayhem for a decade. The four were gunned down in front of Will Fee's Hardware and Mortuary in Fort Pierce in 1924. Hardware stores in the

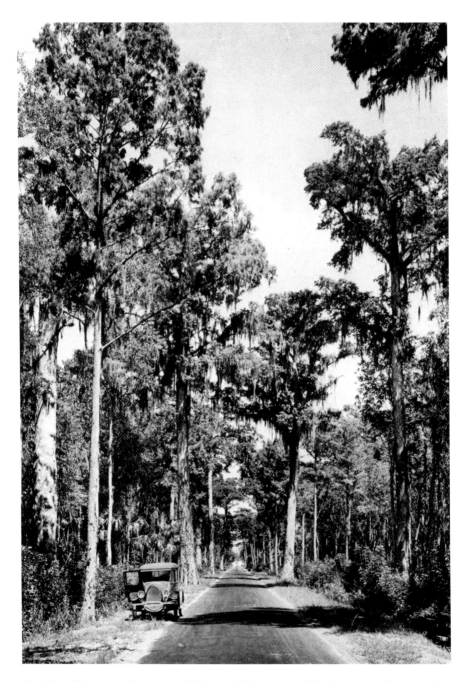

The Dixie Highway, built between 1915 and 1927, connected Florida to the Midwest and allowed tourists to come by the millions. *Florida Archives Photographic Collection.*

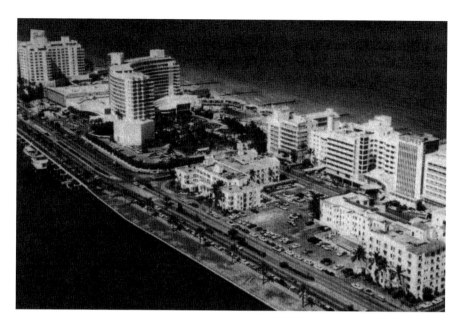

By 1959, Miami's hotel row reigned supreme as the leading tourist spot in Florida. It was often called the American Riviera. *Florida Archives Photographic Collection.*

era sold caskets, and it was a small jump to including a mortuary amid the hammers and farming implements.

In 1924, John Martin won the governorship on a platform of building more roads. That included construction of the Tamiami Trail, which opened in 1928 and connected Tampa and Miami. To show off his state, Martin invited every governor to come and see, and sixteen accepted.

Between 1920 and the 1930s, the state's population soared 52 percent, and tourists were responsible for some of the growth. Many of those who came to visit liked what they saw and stayed.

The airplane brought even more tourists and made it possible to fly directly from East Coast cities to Miami. What became Eastern Airlines began as Florida Airways in 1926 at Paxon Field in Jacksonville with flights to Tampa and Miami. Paxon was one of the state's first airfields and was where the first licensed African American pilot, Bessie Coleman, died in a crash. By 1939, Eastern featured five flights a day from Newark to Miami and two from Chicago to Miami.

National Airlines started in 1934 at a small airport in St. Petersburg. National's purchase of the DC-4 allowed for nonstop jet flights from Miami and New York beginning in 1958.

Even the Wright brothers had a winter home in Aripeka on the west coast and flew airplanes around the rural area, giving thousands their first view of an airplane.

The early tourists came during the winter months—what was known as the "season." The airlines, which had flights year round, needed to fill seats during the summer months and began offering special rates and vacation packages to draw tourists. National called its offer "Piggy Bank Vacations" and drew hundreds of thousands of people. The Boeing 707 cut the flight time, increased the number of flights and drew even more tourists. It was possible to take a flight Friday evening after work, spend two days in the sunshine, and be back at work Monday morning.

Tourists increased to four million in 1946. Many were celebrating the end of World War II, and some came to revisit their old military training camps.

Although the tourists came to every city in the state, Miami was the prime gathering place. The magnificent Fontainebleau Hotel became the symbol for Miami Beach when it opened in 1954 on the grounds of what had been the mansion of Harvey Firestone.

As late as 1977, tourism in Miami still outdrew Orlando four to one, but the opening of Walt Disney World began to lower the margin.

21

FLORIDA GOVERNORS
1868–1950

In 1868, David Walker was replaced by Florida's first Republican governor, Harrison Reed, who came to Florida in 1863 as the tax collector in Jacksonville, appointed by Abraham Lincoln. In 1865, President Andrew Johnson named him postal agent for Florida. As governor, he served under military control. The Republicans retained the governorship in 1872, but with the end of Reconstruction, the Democrats retook control in 1876, when George Drew won by a narrow margin.

The Republican vote decreased as African American voters were disenfranchised. The party won 52 percent of the vote in 1872, 46 percent in 1884, 40 percent in 1888 and 20 percent in 1896.

The Democrats pushed for a rewrite of the Reconstruction constitution, which had dispensed rights. The 1885 constitution sought to limit those rights by dividing power. Limits were placed on the governor's power, a large number of elected offices were created and elected cabinet members held significant power.

For the last quarter of the 1800s, the governors were establishment Democrats, who represented white supremacy and business interests. William Bloxham first ran for governor in 1872 but lost narrowly to the Republican. In 1880, he won easily, and he won another term in 1896. (Florida governors could only serve one consecutive term until the 1970s.)

Bloxham was the governor who sold four million acres to developer Hamilton Disston for twenty-five cents an acre. He also oversaw the first land boom.

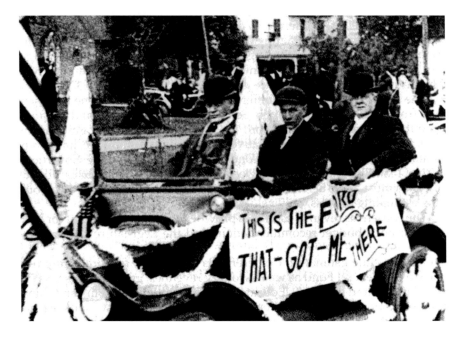

Sidney J. Catts became governor in 1917 on the Prohibition Party ticket. He was the first candidate to campaign by car and rode in one during his inaugural parade. The sign reads, "This Is the FORD That Got Me There." *Florida Archives Photographic Collection.*

The populist movement swept the country in the 1890s, and Florida was caught up in the fever. In 1900, William Sherman Jennings was elected governor on a platform of draining the Everglades and opening it to development. Fortunately for the future of Florida's environment, his plan failed.

As the state grew, the capital in Tallahassee seemed small and remote. In 1900, there was even an election to see if voters wanted to move the capital from Tallahassee. Half of the voters wanted it kept in Tallahassee while almost that percentage favored moving it to either Jacksonville, St. Augustine or Ocala. No city south of Ocala had enough people to even be considered.

In 1904, Florida elected its first true Populist, Napoleon Broward, a man with a colorful past. After his parents died, he was raised by an uncle who ran a steamboat. As a young man he went to work on ships on the St. Johns and eventually became a captain.

When a prison break discredited the Jacksonville sheriff, Broward was appointed to replace him. He became a crusading sheriff, cracking down on the widespread gambling in the city. Broward became a leader of the

FLORIDA SENATORS 1908–1950

In 1908, Duncan U. Fletcher was elected to the U.S. Senate, and eight years later, former governor Park Trammell joined him there. Southern senators usually were elected for life; voters knew that their representatives relied on seniority to block legislation they did not like—usually involving civil rights.

The Great Depression changed politics across the country, sweeping out the old guard and bringing in new faces with new ideas for solving problems. In 1934, Park Trammell was challenged by Claude Pepper, an unknown politician who promised to support the New Deal. Pepper forced Trammell into a runoff and would have won the runoff if not for some ballot stuffing in Tampa. Trammell held on to his seat.

Two years later, Trammell died, and a month later, Fletcher died. Pepper won one seat and a little-known judge from Orlando, Charles O. Andrews, was elected to the other. Andrews served until his death in 1946 and was replaced by Spessard Holland, who served four terms.

Pepper became a national figure, appearing on the cover of *Time* magazine when he ran for reelection in 1938. He became the strongest supporter of the New Deal, which often put him at odds with the voters. He also angered President Harry Truman, who considered him a publicity seeker.

Truman urged Congressman George Smathers to run against Pepper in what became known as one of the nastiest campaigns in history. Smathers won, and his campaign techniques became a model for other candidates running that year, including Richard Nixon in California.

Pepper was out of politics for a dozen years until he was elected to a seat in the House of Representatives in 1962. There, he became a champion of the elderly and of Lyndon Johnson's Great Society. Once again, he was a national figure, appearing on the cover of *Time* magazine.

Straightouts, who were Populists and agrarians. When the pro-business faction took control of the city, Broward was out as sheriff.

Broward returned to steamboats, and in 1896, his steamboat, the *Three Friends*, ran guns to Cuban revolutionaries. His exploits made him famous, especially after the United States declared war on Spain in 1898.

In 1904, he ran for governor, campaigning against the big business interests. He was opposed by the railroad interests and the major newspapers. Broward promised to continue draining the Everglades. He won the primary by just a few hundred votes. As governor, Broward convinced President Theodore Roosevelt to support Everglades drainage.

After leaving the governorship, he ran for United States Senate, but lost to an old ally, Duncan Fletcher. In 1910, he did win a Senate seat, but he died before he could take office.

Albert Gilchrist might have had a career as a soldier, but he could not pass philosophy and flunked out of West Point. He became governor in 1909 and devoted his term to improving healthcare in the state. The state's youngest county is named for him, part of a most unusual political deal. When a county was being carved out of Alachua County, the plan was to name it for Woodrow Wilson, who had died the year before. But at the last minute, someone mentioned that Gilchrist was ill, and it was suggested that naming a county for the former governor would cheer him up.

Florida's most unusual governor was Sidney Catts, who served from 1917 to 1921. He was a Baptist minister in Alabama before moving to Florida in the early 1900s. In 1916, he ran for governor on a racist, anti-liquor and anti-Catholic platform. He told voters that Catholic convents were being used to hide guns, which the Church planned to use to overthrow the government. He seemed to have won the nomination for governor but was declared the loser in a controversial decision. Instead, he ran as the Prohibition Party candidate and won with 43 percent of the vote.

At his inauguration, he carried a revolver because he believed those he called the "pope's men" were planning to assassinate him. He called blacks "an inferior race." He was also the first governor to ride to his inauguration in an automobile.

The legislature ignored his outrageous proposals, which became more extreme. He claimed that the Pope was planning to move the Vatican to a small town near Tampa and close all Protestant churches. He ran for office several more times but always lost.

Governor Cary Hardee presided over Florida during its boom period, 1921 to 1925. The state's population was soaring, new towns were springing up and businesses were prospering. To make sure Florida continued to draw people—especially wealthy people—Hardee pushed through amendments to outlaw the income and inheritance taxes. He also outlawed the leasing of convicts to private businesses, which had been controversial and resulted in deaths.

He was replaced by John Martin, whose timing was terrible. The Florida boom became a bust the same year Martin took office. He had to spend much of his time trying to keep the boom going, traveling throughout the nation to deny there were any problems to an increasingly skeptical people. Martin was able to push through legislation to help finance schools and provide free textbooks for elementary schools.

Doyle Carlton served as governor as the Great Depression hit the nation. Florida was already in a depression, and the national collapse only made things worse. In addition to having to deal with the economy, while he was governor, the state was hit by one of the worst hurricanes in history, and the Mediterranean fruit fly decimated the citrus crop. He failed in subsequent attempts to win election.

The Great Depression made the voters desperate for change, and in 1932, the voters elected David Sholtz, a New York native who scored an upset victory. He worked to blunt the effects of the Depression, but his popularity faded, and a subsequent try for office was unsuccessful.

The next three governors were establishment politicians: Frederick Cone, a banker; Spessard Holland, a leading attorney (the law firm Holland and Knight would become one of the world's largest); and Millard Caldwell, also an attorney.

22

FLORIDA IMMIGRANTS

For the 450 years following the European discovery, Florida's greatest problem was that it had too few people. As late as World War I, vast areas of the state had few people. In 1900, the state's density was less than ten people per square mile—less than Oklahoma. By 2000, there were three hundred people per square mile

It was a difficult task to find people willing to come to a swampy, desolate area with a small economic base.

In 1768, British physician Andrew Turnbull received a land grant of twenty thousand acres from the British government to start a settlement at New Smyrna. He brought 1,500 settlers from Greece, Italy and Minorca to the east coast settlement to start an indigo plantation. It turned into a disaster as disease struck the colony. The living conditions disintegrated, and Turnbull moved to Charleston.

The surviving Minorcans fled to St. Augustine after the colony collapsed. Many of their descendants still live there today.

The British continued trying to bring more people to the colony they acquired in 1763 from the Spanish. The Spanish also gave away huge tracts of land, but neither nation was particularly successful.

The acquisition of Florida by the United States in 1821 brought a wave of new residents, many planters from southern states who brought their slaves.

Still, the population remained tiny. The Civil War did bring deserters from both the Union and Confederate armies, soldiers who knew they would be

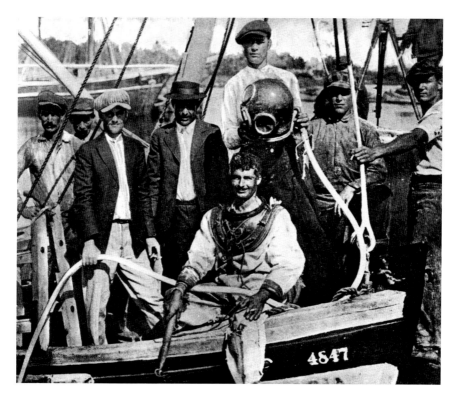

Hundreds of Greek immigrants came to Tarpon Springs to create the sponge industry. *Florida Archives Photographic Collection.*

safe in the nearly empty state. Florida also drew people from southern states anxious to escape the ravages of war.

In 1900, Florida still had only half a million people, about a quarter of the number of people in Alabama. It was the thirty-third-largest state. Nearly all its population lived in a swath between Jacksonville and Pensacola. There were few people in the peninsula, and those who were there were spread out.

Florida looked enviously to the North, where shiploads of immigrants arrived each day. They remained in New York or headed for the industrial cities; few wanted to come to Florida.

The state established a Bureau of Immigration to draw people. The bureau did not last long, but it published a pamphlet titled *The Florida Settler*, which was distributed throughout Europe, and even a newspaper called *Florida Immigrant*, which lasted two years in the late 1870s.

The railroads promoted the state, hoping to sell more tickets and draw farmers who would ship oranges and vegetables to the North. The Atlantic Coast Line Railroad hired poet Sidney Lanier to write about the wonders of Florida.

The enthusiasm to draw people outdrew the reality—one supporter of immigration said, "Florida should be the other Eden." Often Europeans were told that their countries were like Florida.

Many in Florida believed the state should be especially attractive to Italians, who were flocking to the United States. Italians were told that Florida was the "Italy of the South." Chinese workers were told something similar. Those efforts largely failed—only a small number of Italians and Chinese came.

Floridians originally believed the immigrants would work as laborers, replacing the former slaves. Some did come for that purpose, but as the former slaves had learned, the work was backbreaking and the financial rewards small. Sometimes there was no money at the end of the growing season, and there might even be debts to tie the workers to the land.

Many of the immigrants wanted the jobs white Floridians held.

Canadians came to Florida to take the well-paying dock jobs held by white Floridians, touching off anti-Canadian violence in 1876 in Pensacola when Floridians attacked immigrant dockworkers. The legislature moved to allow Canadians to visit but not work; they had to live in Florida for six months before they could work on the docks.

Henry Sanford, who developed orange groves around the community that came to carry his name, formed the Florida Land and Colonization Society. He brought seventy-five Swedish immigrants, but they found that the area was nothing like what they had been led to expect. There were also threats from whites who did not want them taking jobs. They left and formed their own community nearby and named it New Uppsala.

In 1893, some five hundred Danish settlers arrived in St. Lucie County to learn that the land they "bought" belonged to someone else. They faced ruin, but the Florida East Coast Railway stepped in to save their colony. The railroad was not being charitable; Henry Flagler was in the shipping business, and he knew that more farmers meant more goods to ship.

The expansion of the Florida East Coast Railway to South Florida also brought a dozen Danish families from Chicago, followed by another thirty, and they formed Dania—now Dania Beach—as a farming community.

The railroad also brought Japanese immigrants, who settled a colony named Yamato to grow pineapples. At first, the colony thrived; however,

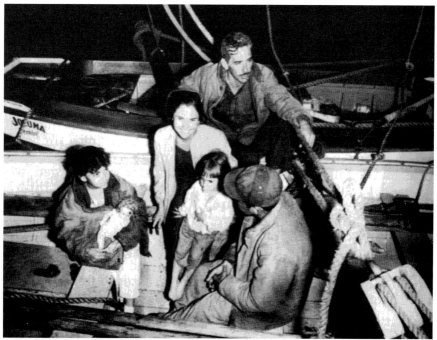

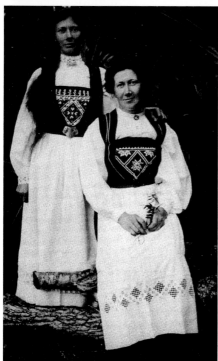

Above: One of thousands of Cuban families to escape to Florida after Fidel Castro came to power, this family landed in Key West on April 11, 1961, just days before the Bay of Pigs invasion. *Florida Archives Photographic Collection.*

Left: Among the immigrants who came to Florida were these two Norwegian women who settled in Polk County in 1912. *Florida Archives Photographic Collection.*

the crop was destroyed in 1908, and the land became Boca Raton. By 1970, only one member of the colony remained, and when he died, he donated his farm as a park in memory of the Yamato Colony.

British settlers arrived in Orlando and created a colony that featured the state's first polo field. They were largely what were known as remittance men, often the second, third, fourth or fifth sons of British nobility or wealth whose fathers sent them away with the understanding that they would receive a regular check. They could often be found at the local post office waiting for their checks.

A group of fifty settlers from Scotland bought land, sight unseen, in Sarasota in 1885, but instead of the thriving community they expected, they found swamps and left.

Greek immigrant John Cocoris brought other Greeks to Tarpon Springs in the early 1900s to start a sponge industry. The Greeks had a method of deep-water diving that made the endeavor particularly successful.

In the 1830s, Bahamian laborers began arriving in Florida. Most were temporary laborers, coming for a few months and then returning home. Most of the early arrivals went to the keys. For some of the Bahamians, it was a round-trip journey. Their ancestors were slaves in Florida who were evacuated to the Bahamas when Spain reclaimed the colony in 1783. Half a century later, their children and grandchildren were back looking for work as free men.

The growth of Miami brought more Bahamians. By 1920, one-fifth of the population of the Bahamas had moved to South Florida. In fact, after half a century of mostly unsuccessful attempts to lure immigrants, Miami turned into a city of immigrants. By 1920, Miami had 30,000 people, including 7,500 foreign immigrants and twice that number from other states.

Turmoil in Latin American nations meant an influx of people to Miami. Cuban exiles, seeking refuge from a succession of governments came to Florida, along with refugees from Mexico, Nicaragua, Haiti, Dominican Republican and a dozen other countries who found new lives in Florida.

23

ORANGES

Christopher Columbus brought the first oranges to the New World from Spain on one of his voyages. The first orange trees in Florida appeared in St. Augustine in the sixteenth century, although there is no way to tell who planted them. The first reference to oranges in Florida came in 1579, when Pedro Menéndez wrote: "There are beginning to be many of the fruits of Spain, such as figs, pomegranates, oranges, grapes in great quantity."

The first groves were in Marion County near Orange Lake, perhaps planted by the Indians with seeds given to them by the Spanish.

The British turned oranges into a cash crop when they took over Florida in 1763. In 1776, two casks of juice and sixty-five thousand oranges were shipped from St. Augustine to England.

Grapefruit came to Florida in 1806, when a French count, Odet Philippe, planted a grove near Tampa. One of the first trees planted by Philippe was still alive in 1925.

It was not until the United States acquired Florida in 1821 that a true citrus industry began to develop. Soon, oranges were being shipped to Charleston, Baltimore, New York and Boston. They were considered a luxury, and many people never tasted one. Well into the twentieth century, they were placed in Christmas stockings as treats.

Oranges were shipped by water in barrels. Because of that, the trees were concentrated around Tampa and St. Augustine.

Orange trees were planted as far north as South Carolina, but an 1835 freeze killed the trees there and pushed the crop back to Florida. The freeze

HENRY SANFORD

Henry Sanford made a fortune during the Civil War. His family made brass tacks in Connecticut before the war, but the war created a huge demand for brass.

The end of the war brought a slowdown in business, and Sanford came to Florida. In 1870, he purchased 12,500 acres on Lake Monroe and named the small settlement after himself.

At first he planted cotton, but caterpillars wiped out his crop. He turned to oranges and found success, creating the modern orange industry. His groves were superior to anything the state had seen and other growers began to follow his techniques.

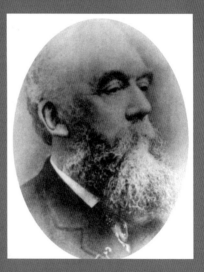

Henry Sanford revolutionized Florida's orange industry. *History Society of Central Florida, Incorporated.*

The project was a drain on his resources, and he took on partners, which only produced disagreements. Finally, he gave up. When he died in 1891, his fortune was almost gone, and he was facing bankruptcy. His once magnificent groves were sold for just $1,000.

But his growing methods revolutionized the industry, and others would profit where he had failed.

also affected North Florida. One pioneer grower wrote, "Trees a hundred years old were killed to the ground." But he noted that within two years, the roots had produced trees and bore fruit.

Zephaniah Kingsley, a leading plantation owner, planted a crop on about four acres and a second small grove nearby to produce sweet oranges, and by 1843, he had planted nearly six thousand trees.

By 1870, Florida was shipping one million boxes of oranges a year to the North. As the transportation system improved and investors realized

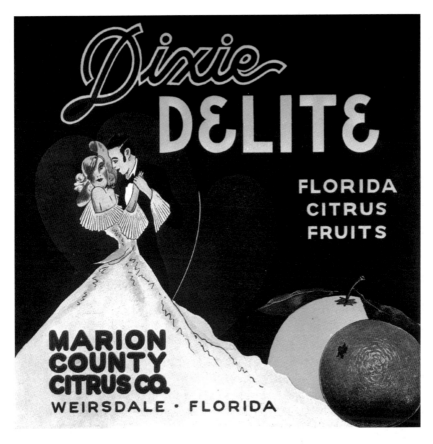

There were hundreds of different orange crate labels representing the various brands and families. *Florida Archives Photographic Collection.*

that money could be made in oranges, the shipments increased and, within twenty-five years, reached five million boxes.

In the 1880s, the railroad reached Orlando and Tampa, making orange transportation easier. An orange picked in Orlando one day could be on a table in New York within a few days.

The outlook for future growth seemed unlimited, but in 1894–95, a ruinous freeze swept through the state. Production declined by 97 percent, and trees were killed by the tens of thousands. The growers began to move farther south to find warmer weather.

Growing oranges is a lengthy process, and it was not until 1910 that production returned to its pre-freeze levels.

THE CRACKERS

For more than one hundred years, the word *cracker* has brought a mixed reaction. Is it a compliment, or is it an insult?

In 1991, the Highlands County School Board voted to name a new school Cracker Trail Elementary School to reflect the county's cattle past. No sooner had the board made the decision than protests began by people who thought the word was derogatory. The board backed down. But then others protested that the term was a tribute to the cowboys, and the name was reinstated.

The word dates back to 1509, and in England, it originally meant a braggart. The word traveled to the New World, where it also had a negative connotation.

The first reference to a cracker in Florida appears in 1790, when the Spanish governor wrote that the crackers in Florida were wild, nomadic and would not heed government authority.

The term gradually was applied to the cowboys who drove cattle and used their bullwhips, which made a loud cracking sound when the tip snapped. While the dictionary still gives it negative connotations, for many Floridians, it is an endearing tribute to the men who were pioneers.

In 1915, it reached 10 million boxes and hit 100 million in 1950. By 1971, the state produced 200 million boxes. Appropriately enough, Orange County became the center of the industry.

As citrus became more important to the economic well-being of Florida, the state and federal governments began research to improve everything from the planting of trees to the shipping of fruit. The Florida State Horticultural Society was established in 1888, and a year later, the Florida Agricultural Experiment States opened. Scientists began to work on citrus breeding and fighting citrus disease.

In 1917, a company in Haines City, southwest of Orlando, began packaging orange juice. No longer did orange buyers have to squeeze oranges to get a glass of juice. It led to even more research to improve the taste and make it more convenient.

The same year the Citrus Research and Education Center was established in Polk County—which was becoming the citrus center of the state.

FINDING PHOSPHATE

In the mid-1800s, phosphate was discovered in England and found to be an excellent fertilizer. Phosphate covers much of the peninsula of Florida, and beginning in the 1880s, a huge industry was created.

In 1880, Dr. C.A. Simmons found some unusual rocks in his quarry near Gainesville. He sent them to Washington and found they were phosphate. He launched the first phosphate mining operation but had little success.

Soon, deposits were found elsewhere. In 1889, Albertus Vogt found high-grade phosphate near the newly created village of Dunnellon in Marion County. Vogt had lived in South Carolina, where phosphate was discovered, and he recognized it in Florida.

He and some partners began buying property and launched the Marion Phosphate Company. The boom turned into a bust within a decade, although many people made their fortune as land went from $1.25 an acre to over $300 an acre.

Captain J. Francis LeBaron of the U.S. Army Corps of Engineers was surveying in 1881 when he discovered phosphate on the Peace River in Polk County. That area became the backbone of the phosphate industry. Five years later, two Orlando businessmen formed a company to begin mining. To acquire land, they came up with a most unusual scheme. They told the landowners they wanted to buy the land to harvest palmetto bushes and then sell the original owners the land back at a lower price. Instead, they removed the phosphate along a forty-three-mile stretch of river.

The Peace River became an economic center. The early "mining" was limited to pebble mining, picking up the phosphate along the riverbank. It was miserable work done with wheelbarrows, picks and shovels. Within a few years, "mining" was done by mules dragging scrapers. By 1888, actual mining had begun. It was cheaper than pebble mining, and within a few years, all pebble mining had stopped.

Eventually, steam shovels were introduced, although the early steam shovels could only hold a small amount of dirt and had to be operated by three men. Still, the three men could replace eighty doing pebble mining.

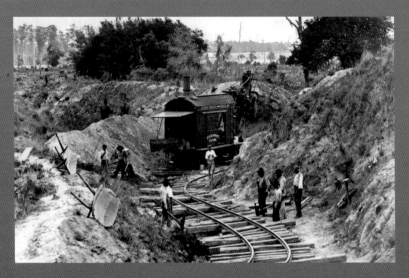

In the 1880s, phosphate was discovered in Marion County and soon became a major industry, supplying much of the world with fertilizer. *Florida Archives Photographic Collection.*

Mining phosphate also involves separating the phosphate from the sand and clay it is mixed with.

The mining company built towns for the workers with houses, hotels, hospitals and even public swimming rooms. The mining towns were in isolated areas, so the mining companies had to build the towns. The largest may have been Brewster, which had a population of 2,500, its own power plant and a movie theater. Founded in 1913, it was abandoned by the company in 1962. The owners of the town, American Cyanamid, turned over the deed to the property to the State of Florida to pay for a judgment against the company for environmental damages the phosphate mining had caused.

For the first half of the twentieth century, phosphate mining was a major industry in Florida. Today, there are three mining companies, and it is still a big business. In all, about 300,000 acres of Florida have been mined.

Phosphate mining became controversial because of the damage to the environment. Large plants were built, belching chemicals into the sky. The phosphate-producing process let fluoride gases escape, damaging crops and threatening cattle.

By the 1960s, there were growing concerns about the pollution and calls for control. The Florida legislature limited chemical emissions because they harmed citrus trees and caused disease in cattle. The creation of the Environmental Protection Agency in the 1970s brought more regulation and demands that the industry reclaim the land it had damaged.

The mines around Polk County are nearly played out, and the companies have moved south. Still, Florida produces most of the fertilizer in the United States and much of the fertilizer shipped to China.

As late as 2013, the Army Corps of Engineers found that creating three phosphate mines and expanding a fourth would destroy nearly 100,000 acres of wetlands and cause damage to fifty miles of streams.

A research lab was built; the research led to the development of frozen concentrate in 1948, and sales soared. Both oranges and the juice could spoil, but frozen concentrate could be stored in freezers and be ready on demand. Frozen concentrate also guaranteed the same, predictable taste.

One of the greatest innovators in the citrus industry was Dr. Philip Phillips, who insisted on being called "Doctor" but had no medical training. He settled in Orlando and became the largest grower in the nation. But his real contribution was the research and promotion he undertook. He created a demand for oranges by advertising. In 1931, he came up with what became known as the "flash" process, which removed the metallic taste that was caused by the acidity in the orange. He even got an endorsement for orange juice from the American Medical Association.

In the 1980s, three things began to affect the orange industry: weather, people and Brazil. The South American country became a major citrus producer, and by 2014, it was producing three times as many oranges as Florida. For Brazil, it was a cash crop—99 percent of the production was for export—rather than for consumption at home.

Other countries also joined the rush to grow oranges, and Florida's percentage of the world's orange production fell to 20 percent. Florida also

THE COWBOYS

As they had sugar, the Spanish brought cows to Florida. After his initial discovery of Florida in 1513, Ponce de León waited seven years before returning. When he did come back, he brought with him hundreds of settlers along with seven Andalusian cattle—the ancestors of the Texas Longhorns.

Ponce de León's expedition ended in disaster, and the cattle were left behind. Other expeditions, led by Hernando de Soto and Tristán de Luna also brought cattle, and though their expeditions also ended in failure, the cows remained.

The Spanish did not find gold or silver in Florida, their attempts to grow crops were largely unsuccessful and it appeared there was little economic opportunity for them. The cattle industry proved to be the exception, and by 1700, there were twenty-five ranches with 1,620 head of cattle. One ranch, near present-day Gainesville, had 770.

In the eighteenth century, the Seminole Indians began raising cattle, and the Seminole chief Micanopy had a herd of several thousand.

One of the problems the cattlemen faced was transportation. Florida was isolated, and cows had to be driven to Alabama or Georgia or shipped to Cuba. The attraction of Cuba was that the cattle were paid for in gold.

During the Civil War, Florida cattle were in high demand by the Union and the Confederacy. Because Florida was far removed from the fighting, cattle could be raised in relative safety.

The Civil War severely reduced the number of cows in Florida, and it was not until the 1920s that the herds returned to their pre—

lost its dominant position in tangerine production and led in only one citrus crop, grapefruit.

Florida remained the top state for citrus production, producing 63 percent of the citrus crop, twice as much as California.

In the 1980s, there were more tree-killing freezes. But this time, the growers had a choice: they could sell their land at a handsome profit, or they could replant. In the area around Orlando, the developers swooped in and

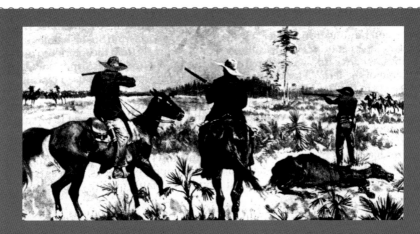

Harper's Monthly sent famed western artist Frederick Remington to Florida to draw and write about the state's cowboys. In this drawing, cowboys shoot it out in a range war. *Florida Archives Photographic Collection.*

Civil War levels. Until 1949, cows in Florida were allowed to roam free, often strolling onto highways and sometimes causing fatal accidents—to the cows and the drivers.

The 1900s also saw advances in raising cattle involving irrigation systems, improved grass and disease control. New types of cattle were brought into Florida—Brahma in the 1890s and English breeds after 1900. Still the original cows—known as the cracker cow—remained the mainstay of the Florida cattle industry.

The cattlemen organized the Cattlemen's Association in 1934 to improve breeds, conduct research into diseases, market their product and lobby the legislature for favorable treatment.

built thousands of homes, shopping centers and businesses. At one time, the 226-foot-tall Citrus Tower located north of Orlando was one of the major tourist attractions in Florida, overlooking thousands of acres of orange trees. Today, it overlooks thousands of homes.

As citrus became a big business, large companies swept in and bought smaller firms, or the smaller firms grew. Tropicana was founded in 1947 by Anthony Rossi in Bradenton. Rossi emigrated from Italy. He began by packaging citrus gift baskets and then produced frozen concentrate. In 1952, he purchased a canning company and abandoned his gift boxes. In 1978, Rossi sold the company to Beatrice Foods, which sold it to Seagrams, which sold it to Pepsi in 1998. The company became the state's largest buyer of oranges.

Minute Maid began in 1945 as Florida Foods. A Boston company developed a method of turning orange juice into powder with the idea of selling it to the army for use during World War II. The war ended before the powder could be produced, and the company temporarily abandoned its plans for a powder. Instead, it pioneered frozen concentrate and produced its first product in 1946.

The company was so small, it could not advertise, and the firm's president went door to door handing out samples. It adopted the Minute Maid name in 1949.

Singer Bing Crosby was hired to promote the juice, and sales soared. In 1960, the company was sold to Coca-Cola.

24

FLORIDA COLLEGES

For more than a century, there has been a debate over which college was the first in Florida. Florida Southern College in Lakeland traces its roots to 1856, when the South Florida Institute opened in downtown Orlando. A series of moves and name changes brought it to Lakeland in 1922. Today, it is known throughout the world for its magnificent campus designed by Frank Lloyd Wright.

Rollins College also claims to be the first, starting in 1885 in Winter Park and keeping the same name and location.

The early Florida colleges were usually church related—Florida Southern was Methodist, and Rollins was Congregational—and the state government resisted opening colleges. Stetson University in DeLand also began in the 1880s, named for John Stetson, the hat king, and backed by the Baptist Church.

The state first considered entering the field of higher education in 1828, when territorial governor William Duval proposed creating a college, but the legislature did nothing until 1851, when two seminaries were authorized—one in the peninsula, the other in the panhandle.

The East Florida Seminary was opened in Ocala in 1851, a small school with a combination of high school and college courses. It is recognized as the predecessor of the University of Florida. Tallahassee was selected as the home of the West Florida Seminary, and a century later became Florida State University.

The East Florida Seminary closed at the start of the Civil War, and when it reopened in 1866, it was moved to Gainesville. The Florida Agricultural

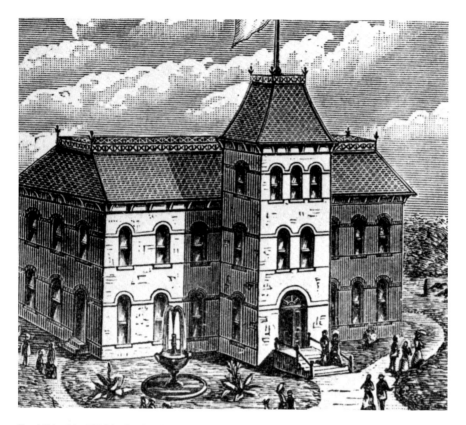

Established in 1856 in Ocala, the East Florida Seminary became the University of Florida in Gainesville after the Civil War. *Florida Archives Photographic Collection.*

College was established in Lake City in 1884 and became the state's first land-grant college. In 1903, it became the University of Florida.

In 1905, the Buckman Act reorganized the state's schools of higher education. The University of Florida at Lake City, the St. Petersburg Normal and Industrial School in St. Petersburg, the South Florida Military College in Bartow and the East Florida Seminary in Gainesville were merged into the University of the State of Florida to provide higher education for white males. Some white women were admitted beginning in 1924, and it became totally coeducational after World War II. The orange and black colors of East Florida Seminary, and the blue and white colors of the Lake City school were combined to become the orange and blue of the University of Florida.

The law also established the State Normal School for Colored Students, which became Florida A&M University, and the Florida Female College,

MARY BETHUNE

It would have been impossible to look at five-year-old Mary Jane McLeod picking cotton in 1884 in Mayesville, South Carolina, and imagine that one day she would be a guest at the White House and found a university that would provide an education to thousands of African Americans.

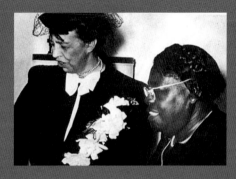

Mary Bethune counted Eleanor Roosevelt among her many influential friends. *Florida Archives Photographic Collection.*

She was the child of slaves, the fifteenth of seventeen children, and some of her brothers and sisters were former slaves. With the help of some neighbors, she was able to gain a high school education. She won a scholarship to Barber-Scotia College and spent a year in Chicago studying to be a missionary.

She returned to the South to do social work. Along with her husband, she ran a mission school in Palatka. Her husband returned to South Carolina, but the couple never divorced.

She taught in Georgia and South Carolina and then moved to Daytona to start a school for girls. She had only $1.50, but the town dump was next door and became the source for many of the furnishings for her school. Furniture was made from crates; for pencils, she used burnt wood, and ink came from elderberry juice.

In the Jim Crow era, she made friends with many of the white residents of the town who helped her. She was also able to meet some of the most influential people in the country, including James Gamble of Proctor & Gamble, oil king John D. Rockefeller and Thomas White of the White Sewing Machine fortune.

She became an advisor to four presidents: Calvin Coolidge, Herbert Hoover, Franklin Roosevelt and Harry Truman. She became friends with Eleanor Roosevelt, who introduced her to other donors.

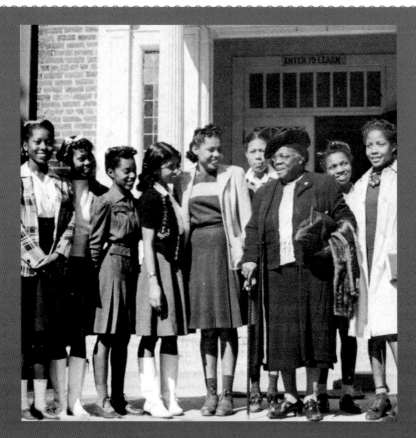

Mary Bethune had only $1.50 when she started what became Bethune-Cookman University. She posed with students in front of White Hall, donated by Thomas White, the founder of the White Sewing Machine Company. *Florida Archives Photographic Collection.*

In 1931, the Methodist Church merged her school with the Cookman Institute, a boys' school, and formed Bethune-Cookman College. Despite the name, it remained a secondary school with two years of college.

Roosevelt called on Bethune frequently on issues of importance to African Americans, and her absence hurt the college. By 1941, it was a four-year-college. She stepped down the following year because of declining health. She died in 1955. In 2007, Bethune-Cookman became a university.

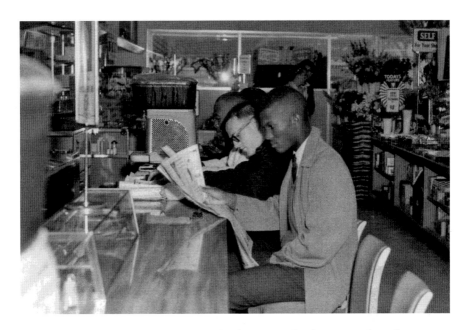

Students at Florida A&M University organized protests at lunch counters throughout Tallahassee to force integration. They faced violence from whites and arrests by police. *Florida Archives Photographic Collection.*

which became Florida State University after World War II. The Florida School for the Deaf and Blind was created in St. Augustine.

Those schools served the state until after World War II. As a result of the GI Bill of Rights, which gave veterans money to attend college, and the postwar baby boom, state officials realized that the state schools would soon be overwhelmed.

Beginning with the University of South Florida in Tampa in 1957, the state created nine more schools.

The state's first two-year college was St. Petersburg Junior College, which opened in 1927. In 1939, the legislature approved the creation of two-year schools, but nothing happened until 1947, when St. Petersburg Junior College became part of the state system and three new schools were approved in Palm Beach, Pensacola and Marianna.

In all, twenty-eight community colleges were opened. In 2001, schools in St. Petersburg, Fort Myers, Miami and Marianna were allowed to issue four-year degrees, and soon others followed. Miami Dade College has become a sprawling institution with eight campuses and over 161,000 students. What began as Dade County Junior College in 1960 is also home to the Miami

Book Fair International, which has become one of the largest book festivals in the world.

The University of Miami was a product of the land boom of the 1920s. George Merrick founded Coral Gables as an upscale residential community, and he and others believed that a college would enhance the community. In 1926, 550 students enrolled, but when the land boom collapsed, the school barely survived. The school was forced into bankruptcy and seemed headed toward collapse. But it survived and grew and today is the largest private university in the Southeast.

For most of Florida's history, opportunities for African Americans to obtain a college education were very limited. Florida A&M University in Tallahassee was the only state-supported school for African Americans, but by the 1920s, it tended to emphasize vocational courses rather than a strong academic program.

25

MAKING MUSIC

The first people to make music in Florida were the natives who played a variety of instruments and sang along with the music. When Pánfilo de Narváez came to Florida in 1528, he encountered Indians playing reed instruments. Near present-day Ocala, Hernando de Soto saw Indians who used conch shells as trumpets. When Pedro Menéndez came to settle St. Augustine, he had dinner with the Calusa tribe and was entertained by "two fifers and drummers, three trumpeters, one harp, one vihuela de arco (a guitar-shaped instrument played with a bow) and one psaltery (string instrument)." There was also a singer. Menéndez staged his own entertainment, having some of his men sing during the dinner.

As early as 1599, Spanish priests in Florida were teaching religious songs to the Indians. As St. Augustine was settled in the late 1500s and early 1600s, the music became more sophisticated and featured chamber music, vocal arrangements and even keyboard music.

Fifers and drummers who accompanied the Menéndez expedition were paid six ducats a month, a respectable salary.

When the British attacked St. Augustine in 1586, they brought with them their own musicians who played as the British burned the town. When the British took over Florida in 1763, two centuries of Catholic religious music all but disappeared and was replaced by the music of the Church of England. As a result of the British occupation, the minuet was heard at St. Augustine social functions.

The Spanish regained Florida in 1783, and once again, their music returned. The reign lasted less than four decades before Florida became an American

STEPHEN FOSTER

One of Florida's two state songs was the third choice for the man who wrote it, Stephen Foster. Foster eventually named his song "Way Down Upon the Swanee River," better known as "Old Folks at Home." He lived in Pittsburgh in 1851, where he wrote a song he called "Way Down Upon the Pee Dee River," the name of a South Carolina river. But he wasn't happy with the title.

He also considered naming it for the Yazoo River in Mississippi. An atlas was consulted, and somebody shouted "Suwannee." He had never been to Florida, but he liked the name. He needed two syllables, so he changed the pronunciation and spelling from "Suwannee" to "Swanee."

In 1935, the Florida legislature adopted the song as the official state song replacing "Florida, My Florida."

Today, the song is considered offensive, although a few word changes over the years have made it more palatable for official state functions. Foster's lyrics painted a bucolic picture of plantation life in the days of slavery: "Still longing for de old plantation, And for de old folks at home."

Although Foster's chorus contains the line, "Oh darkies, how my heart grows weary," when the new Florida capitol building was dedicated in 1978, the line was changed in the official program to read, "Oh brothers, how my heart grows weary."

At Governor Jeb Bush's second inauguration in 2003, the words were changed from "still longing for the old plantation," to "still longing for my old connection." At his 2007 inauguration, Charlie Crist dropped the song entirely.

An attempt to have a new official state song resulted in more confusion as the state ended up with two official songs, including Foster's controversial one. The second is "I Am Florida," which is one of the state's best-kept secrets, even though it was recognized by the legislature in 2013.

territory. The official ceremony took place on July 17, 1821, and an American band played "The Star-Spangled Banner," and the American flag was raised.

William Duval, the first territorial governor, often sang for his friends. His favorites were the songs "My Boy Tommy" and "Tam O'Shanter."

As Florida grew, it seemed that music was everywhere, not only in churches but also at dances, concerts, in homes and even on ships that docked at Jacksonville and Pensacola. Florida became sophisticated enough to have operas.

Before the Civil War, there were concerts by black entertainers who sang African American ballads and white entertainers who used burnt cork to make their faces black and imitate black performers. They gave concerts throughout Florida.

The Civil War brought military music, mainly marches as the soldiers went off to war and drums as the soldiers drilled, and of course, "Dixie" was heard everywhere. Union troops occupied Pensacola during the war and a regiment of the colorfully dressed New York Zouave soldiers offered a night of entertainment for the community. The show featured soldiers singing songs such as "Get Along Home Yaller Gals," "Seeing Nelly Home" and "The Boy with the Auburn Hair."

Perhaps because of its location, or its shifting population, Florida has been home to many different types of music over the years.

It has strong country music roots as evidenced by two of country music's early stars, Mel Tillis and Slim Whitman. Tillis was born in Dover in 1932, and after a stint in the military, he began writing and then singing songs. In 2012, President Barack Obama awarded Tillis the National Medal of Arts. Whitman was born in Tampa, and his yodeling and high falsetto became an early staple of country music beginning in the 1950s. His hits "Indian Love Call" and "Rose Marie" became country and western classics.

Whitman toured with Elvis Presley early in Presley's career. Presley sang in Florida with two country music tours, one headlined by Hank Snow and the other by Andy Griffith. After he became a star, Presley returned to film *Follow That Dream* in Ocala and Yankeetown. Singer John Anderson from Apopka had a string of country hits including "Swingin'," "Seminole Wind" and "Black Sheep."

Jazz great Cannonball Adderley was born in Tampa in 1928, and his family moved to Fort Lauderdale. His nickname was given to him by his friends at Dillard High School who called him "cannibal" because of his huge appetite. Cannibal became Cannonball. His parents took jobs as teachers at Florida A&M University, and he moved to Tallahassee in the early 1940s. He started playing the saxophone with Miles Davis and then formed his own group.

Singer Billy Daniels, best known for his song "That Old Black Magic," was born in Jacksonville and went to New York to attend Columbia University. He

RAY CHARLES

Ray Charles had a life filled with great success and great tragedy. He was born in Georgia, but his family moved to Greenville, a small town in the Florida Panhandle. His mother was a sharecropper, and his father worked as a railroad repairman. He played around the shacks where blacks lived in Greenville and watched the men at a nearby café play the piano.

Tragedy first struck when he saw his brother drown in a laundry tub, a memory that haunted him the rest of his life. When he was five, he began to lose his sight, and by the time he was seven, he was blind. His mother sent him to the Florida School for the Deaf and Blind in St. Augustine. While he was there, his parents died. He learned to play the piano and performed on a local radio station.

He came to hate the school and was expelled when he was fifteen years old. His final report card carried the words "Unsatisfactory pupil." Charles said that he refused to play the guitar because the school was training blind black students to be street beggars. "You can't play piano on a street corner," he said years later.

He joined a band in Jacksonville, but the band ran out of money, leaving Charles stranded. He moved to Orlando, where he played in several bands, including a country and western band for about year. He remembered buying his first record player in Orlando and wearing his first pair of sunglasses, which became his trademark.

Charles had trouble paying his rent, and a kindly landlady carried him when he could not pay. He got a friend to get a map and find the spot as far away from Florida as possible. He picked Seattle.

began working at a nightclub as a dishwasher, then a singing waiter and finally as a singer. He also became the first African American to have a network television show when he starred in *The Billy Daniels Show* on ABC in 1952.

The rock-and-roll era produced Johnny Tillitson, who grew up in Jacksonville and Palatka. He began performing at Palatka Senior High School and became a regular on a local television show in Jacksonville. At the University of Florida, he entered a Pet Milk talent contest and was invited to Nashville to sing on the Grand Ole Opry. His hit "Poetry in Motion" in 1960 reached number two on

American music charts, and he followed it two years later with *It Keeps Right on A-Hurtin'*.

Jim Morrison was born in Melbourne, where his father was an admiral. His family moved to New Mexico when he was a child, but he returned to attend St. Petersburg Junior College and then Florida State University. He left FSU after being arrested for pulling a prank while drunk at a football game. Morrison died of a drug overdose when he was twenty-seven. He was inducted into the Rock and Roll Hall of Fame in 1993.

The Lynyrd Skynyrd Band started in 1964 in Jacksonville as the Noble Five and became famous with its songs "Sweet Home Alabama" and "Free Bird." In 1977, at the peak of the group's success, three members of the band died in a plane crash. The surviving members re-formed in 1987. The band was inducted into the Rock and Roll Hall of Fame in 2006.

The Allman Brothers Band was also formed in Jacksonville and became a leader in the genre that became known as southern rock. Bandleader Duane Allman was killed in a 1971 motorcycle accident, and bassist Berry Oakley died the following year in another motorcycle accident. The band carried on and, in 1973, had its greatest hit, "Ramblin' Man." The band was inducted into the Rock and Roll Hall of Fame in 1995.

Gram Parsons of Winter Haven had a short but influential career as his music combined rock and country. He performed with a number of groups, including the Byrds. Drugs damaged his health, and he died at the age of twenty-six.

Florida was also the home to the boy band movement. Groups such as the Backstreet Boys and 'N Sync started in Orlando. One of the 'N Sync members, Justin Timberlake, went on to have his own film and music career.

The influx of immigrants into South Florida has given the music a decidedly Latin flavor best exemplified by Cuban-born Gloria Estefan. Her father was a soldier and bodyguard for Cuban dictator Fulgencio Batista. Her family fled to Miami as a result of the revolution that overthrew Batista. She married Emilio Estefan, the leader of the Miami Sound Machine, in 1978.

Gloria Estefan became increasingly popular, and eventually the band's name was changed to Gloria Estefan and the Miami Sound Machine.

In the 1970s, Miami became a recording center as Fleetwood Mac recorded *Rumours* and the Eagles recorded *Hotel California*. And in the Florida Keys, Jimmy Buffett created his own sound that made him a legend.

26

SPACE AGE FLORIDA

In the 1800s, writer Jules Verne wrote of a flight to the moon in *From the Earth to the Moon*. In his fantasy, three men were launched from Florida on a journey to the moon. A century later, his wild imagination proved amazingly accurate.

Americans' first efforts to conquer space began at White Sands Proving Ground in New Mexico, and the space program might well have stayed there had it not been for some very unusual problems. The site was too small, and there were concerns that if the missile went astray it would hit a populated area. The fallback site was El Centro, California, but the Mexican government said that a misfire could strike Mexicali across the border.

The federal government realized that the launch site needed to be on the water so that errant missiles would fall into the ocean. Scientists found that being closer to the equator made launches easier.

The choice was the Banana River Naval Air Station near Titusville. In 1949, President Harry S. Truman authorized a testing facility at what was later named Patrick Air Force Base.

In July 1950, the first missile was launched, a V-2 rocket confiscated from the Germans combined with a WAC corporal rocket. The military operated the base until 1958, when the National Aeronautics and Space Administration (NASA) took over. Thousands of additional acres were added to what became the Kennedy Space Center.

The space program received a major boost in 1957, when the Russians sent the satellite Sputnik into space. The space race between Russia and the United

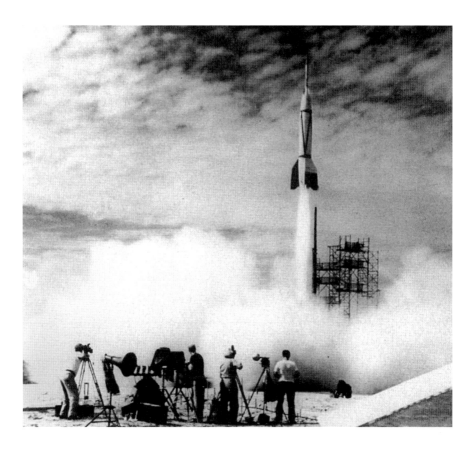

In 1950, the space age began with the launch of a rocket from Cape Canaveral. Known as *Bumper 2*, it was a two-stage rocket combining a German V-2 missile base with a WAC Corporal rocket. *Florida Archives Photographic Collection.*

States was underway. In 1961, President John Kennedy announced that the United States would put a man on the moon by the end of the decade.

In May of that year, Alan Shepard became the first man in space, and a year later, John Glenn became the first American to orbit the earth, flying around the world three times. The spacemen became known as astronauts.

Glenn and Shepard were part of Project Mercury, which ended with Gordon Cooper going around the earth twenty-two times in thirty-four hours. Mercury was followed by the Gemini Program, which advanced the space program with larger spacecraft and two-man crews. Edward H. White became the first man to walk in space during Gemini. Gemini showed that astronauts could stay in space for fourteen days—enough time to travel to the moon and back.

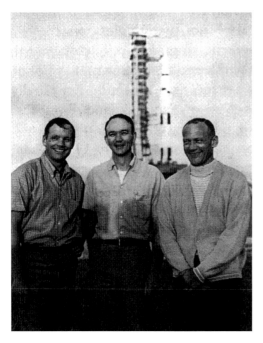

(From left to right) Neil Armstrong, Michael Collins and Buzz Aldrin pose in front of the spacecraft that took them to the moon two weeks after this image was taken. *Florida Archives Photographic Collection.*

The final step in the race to the moon was the Apollo program. On July 29, 1969—five months before the deadline set by President Kennedy. Neil Armstrong and Edwin Aldrin walked on the moon while Mike Collins orbited above them.

The space program brought thousands of people to the space center, including scientists, engineers, technicians and computer experts.

When the Apollo program ended, NASA sought a way to keep the manned-space program alive and came up with the space shuttle. NASA called it a new era in space travel. The spacecraft was launched like a rocket, flown in space like a spacecraft, and landed like an airplane.

In 1986, the Space Shuttle *Challenger* broke apart just seventy-three seconds after launching from Cape Kennedy. The disaster killed all seven crew members. The shuttle program ended in 2011, ending manned flight.

27

THE 1920s

World War I saw the beginning of the Florida boom. There was a new instrument of war, the airplane, and the perfect place to train pilots was Florida. A year before the war began in Europe, the United States opened a flight school in Pensacola. Once the war started, forty-two thousand Floridians entered military service. Even Fort Myers resident Thomas Edison was involved; he went to Key West to work on improving depth charges. On September 26, 1918, the Coast Guard cutter USS *Tampa* was struck by a torpedo as it sailed in British waters. The entire crew was lost, including twenty-three sailors from Tampa.

As with the Seminole Wars, the Civil War and the Spanish-American War, World War I brought people into Florida who decided to remain. It was the beginning of the biggest period of growth in Florida history.

The 1920s created a new Florida, one of tourists, millionaires and housing developments. The rise of the automobile and the construction of highways gave millions of Americans a way to reach the warm weather. The American labor system was changing, and workers had vacations that gave them the time to head to Florida

In 1920, more than 63 percent of Floridians lived on farms or in small towns of fewer than 2,500 people. By 1940, more than 55 percent lived in the cities. The state's three largest cities—St. Petersburg, Jacksonville and Miami—collectively contained one-third of the population of the state.

Florida real estate was cheap and abundant and in reach for Americans who wanted a vacation home or to make a permanent move. Buying and selling land

CARL FISHER

Carl Fisher was one of the most remarkable men of the twentieth century—an inventor, innovator and developer who left us with everything from the Indianapolis 500 to Miami Beach.

He started with a small bicycle shop in Indiana, and in 1904, he acquired rights to manufacture the first automobile headlights. Nearly every early automobile maker used his headlamps. He sold the company a decade later for $9 million—a fortune then.

Fisher was a major force behind the early national highways, including the Lincoln Highway, the first coast-to-coast highway. He also built the Indianapolis Motor Speedway.

He developed the Dixie Highway, stretching from the upper Midwest to Miami. The highway brought Fisher to Miami, where he became interested in Miami Beach.

He moved to Miami to live on his fortune; however, he became restless and a swampy area across the bay drew his attention. The narrow peninsula attracted John Collins, who grew avocados but had trouble getting them to the market. Collins began building a bridge but ran out of money. Fisher stepped in with a loan, and Collins gave him two hundred acres on Miami Beach.

It was not much of a gift, largely a swampy jungle; still, Fisher plunged in and bought another two hundred acres. His friends thought he was crazy, but Fisher promised to build "the prettiest little city in the world right here."

He began dredging and filling and made significant progress, but he also began running out of money. Just when it appeared that Fisher would have to declare bankruptcy, the Florida land boom began. Soon Fisher's worthless land was worth a fortune.

Fisher had done more than wait for the land boom; he had helped create it. In addition to lobbying for the Dixie Highway that brought millions of tourists to Florida, he was a master promoter. He created well-publicized stunts to draw even more people. His ultimate stunt came when he entertained president-elect Warren G. Harding at his luxury hotel. When Harding played golf, Fisher rented a baby elephant to serve as Harding's caddy. The picture made front pages around the world.

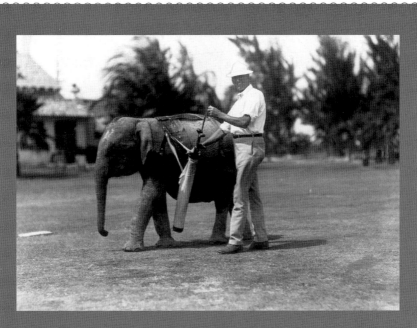

In one of the greatest publicity stunts of all time, Miami Beach developer Carl Fisher had an elephant named Rosie serve as a caddy for president-elect Warren G. Harding. *Florida Archives Photographic Collection.*

By 1925, at the height of the land boom, his land went from worthless to worth millions of dollars.

Miami Beach was a success, and most thought Fisher would retire as he had planned to do twelve years earlier. Instead, he plunged in again, buying ten thousand acres on the tip of Long Island, hoping to repeat his success of Miami Beach.

But Fisher's luck was running out. A 1926 hurricane in Florida dampened tourism and killed the Florida land boom. Then, the stock market crash of 1929 destroyed his dreams for a resort at Montauk. He lost everything, spending his last years in a small house and walking the beach he once owned in his blue blazer and white trousers.

THE CIRCUS KING

When John and Charles Ringling came to Sarasota in 1910, there were just 810 hearty souls in the isolated village. Despite the drawbacks, the brothers saw possibilities in the area and purchased sixty-seven thousand acres as an investment, later to be a winter headquarters for their world-famous circus.

When John Ringling and his wife, Mable, first arrived, they purchased a frame house to live in. In 1925, they began construction on their fabulous mansion called Cá d'Zan.

The Mediterranean Revival house was inspired by Mable's favorite Venetian hotels. The mansion cost $1.5 million—about $40 million today—with an additional $400,000 spent on furnishing the lavish home. John Ringling began assembling a large collection of fine art from Europe, including a large collection of works by Rubens.

The next year, John Ringling decided that Sarasota would become the winter home of his circus. The circus and its performers moved to two hundred acres on the east side of town. They stayed there from late November to early March, when the circus loaded its equipment and people on trains and headed for the annual opening in New York.

At one time, John Ringling was thought to be the fifth-richest man in the country, but financial mistakes, an unhappy second

could be a chance to make a fortune. A few hundred dollars could be turned into thousands of dollars overnight. It seemed as though anyone could get rich.

As for the rich, Florida offered not only warm weather but also financial advantages. To lure wealthy people to Florida, the legislature passed a constitutional amendment outlawing the income tax and the inheritance tax. Even people who spent 99 percent of their time somewhere else could build a home in Florida and avoid income taxes back in their home state.

Florida land salesmen had great help from Northern newspapers, which published hundreds of stories about the money to be made in Florida. The result was that two-thirds of the land sold in Florida was by mail to people who had never seen it and had no idea whether the land they were buying was oceanfront or underwater. To meet the demand, Florida relaxed its rules

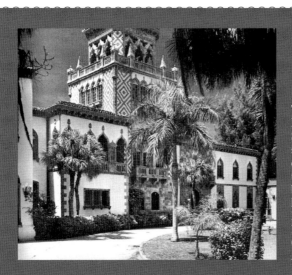

The sprawling Ringling home in Sarasota featured some of the most expensive artwork in the world. Sarasota became the winter home of the Ringling Brothers and Barnum & Bailey Circus. *Florida Archives Photographic Collection.*

marriage and the Great Depression combined to break him. His wife, Mable, died in 1929, and though the following year he remarried, the marriage was unhappy. He lost everything except his home and art collection.

He died a lonely man in 1936 with just $311 left in the bank.

He left his mansion and the art collection to the state of Florida. At first, little was done with the property as the state fought with Ringling's creditors. In 2000, the property was transferred to Florida State University and was restored to its original glory.

on real estate salespeople. There was a sense that if one didn't buy today, tomorrow would be too late.

By 1922, the *Miami Herald* was the heaviest newspaper in the country, loaded with page after page of property listings for sale. When paperboys threw it on front porches, it made a thunderous thud that could wake homeowners.

Developers often erected a fancy entrance, put stakes where they promised to build roads and began selling lots. Sometimes the developers didn't even own the land but merely an option to buy it if they were successful at selling lots.

A new industry was created, populated by young men called binder boys. The binder boys stationed themselves at property that was for sale. They would accept a down payment, or binder, to hold the property for thirty days. The checks could take weeks to clear, but the binder receipts themselves

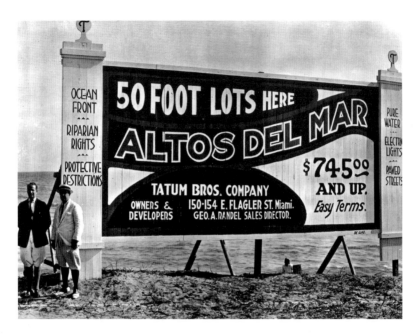

For $745, it was possible to buy a lot on Miami Beach in the 1920s. Today, homes in the development sell for millions of dollars. *Florida Archives Photographic Collection.*

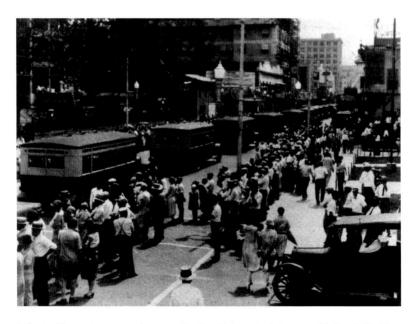

A fleet of buses transported perspective land buyers to lots around Miami. *Florida Archives Photographic Collection.*

BARRON COLLIER

Barron Collier was already wealthy when he came to Florida. The child of a poor Memphis family, he dropped out of school when he was just sixteen.

He went to work for a railroad but soon started his own business. He was a millionaire by the time he was twenty-six. His road to riches was selling advertising on trains and streetcars, a new concept that quickly caught on.

In 1911, he came to Fort Myers for the first time. For just $100,000, he bought nearby Useppa Island, but that was just the start. He went on to purchase 1.3 million acres in Southwest Florida, making him the largest landowner in the state. His landholdings were so vast that the state named a county for him. He said, "When I first came here on holiday with Juliet [his wife], I never expected that I would buy a whole region of it, nor did I expect to pay for the new Tamiami Trail, or half the things I've done. But I really didn't expect to have a whole county named for me."

The Tamiami Trail was a massive undertaking, connecting Southwest Florida to Southeast Florida for the first time.

The Great Depression slowed the development, but he was able to keep all of his property and pass it along to his son when he died in 1939.

Today a list of the family holdings would fill a small book. There is the land, shopping centers, office parks, residential communities, hotels, cattle, oil and minerals. They also have vast landholdings in Arizona.

One of their major efforts in conservation has been to save the Florida panther, which has been threatened by development and speeding cars.

became a form of currency to be used until the checks cleared. Often, the buyers resold the property before the thirty days was up—at a profit.

Not only were rules for real estate salespeople relaxed—or rather, the already lax requirements were made even easier—state banks found they could do anything and not worry about state regulators. The legislature approved rules for horse- and dog racing, but casinos and illegal saloons hardly needed legal permission to operate in Miami, where law enforcement looked the other way.

Prohibition helped the Florida economy. The primary support for the constitutional amendment outlawing liquor had come from the South. Within Florida, there was strong support for the measure, mostly from rural areas. While the voters supported Prohibition, the tourists did not. They wanted a drink, and Bimini and Cuba were nearby.

The two islands meant that liquor was just an hour or two away—and not the stuff that was made in bathtubs, but real liquor, imported from Europe or made in the islands like rum. The money involved was too good to pass up, and hundreds of police and other public officials took bribes to look the other way.

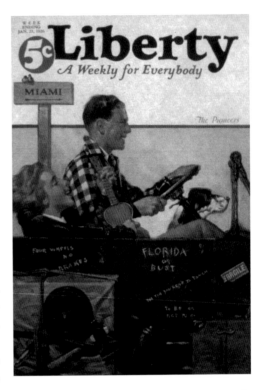

A 1926 cover of *Liberty* magazine told the story of "Florida or Bust." *Library of Congress.*

With its thousands of miles of empty coastline, Florida offered the rumrunners the perfect landing place. By 1921, there were nine giant warehouses on Grand Bahama Island—sixty miles from Palm Beach—packed with liquor meant for sale in Florida. Soon, Florida had more airport runways than any other southern state even though it had the smallest population. There were more crop-dusting planes than any other southern state—perfect for bringing in illegal liquor.

The new communities sometimes did not even require land. David Davis began in Tampa with some mud and turned it into Davis Islands. He tried to repeat his magic in St. Augustine but went broke and ended up committing suicide.

Barron Collier developed Naples and Marco Island as winter resorts and ended up with a county named for him. Carl Fisher took another hunk of swampland and turned it into Miami Beach. George Merrick bought 1,100

THOMAS EDISON

Beginning in the 1880s, Florida became a mecca for wealthy industrialists and tycoons who flocked to the grand hotels in Jacksonville, St. Augustine and later Palm Beach.

Inventor Thomas Edison was drawn to the remote fishing village of Fort Myers, which he first visited in 1885. While cruising along the Florida coast, he saw the small town with just 349 residents. He docked his boat and went ashore. He built a home and a laboratory and carried out some of his research there. He also built one of the first concrete swimming pools in Florida, although he never used it.

After his first wife died, he remarried and went to Fort Myers for his honeymoon. His friend Henry Ford liked the town so much that he built a home near Edison's. Their fame helped attract others and turned the village into a city.

acres of citrus trees and built nearby Coral Gables. He hired three-time presidential nominee William Jennings Bryan as his pitchman to use his magnificent voice to convince people to buy lots the way he had convinced them to vote for him. Bryan mixed Bible lessons with property pitches. Merrick even started his own college to draw customers—the University of Miami.

Hollywood and Boca Raton sprang up, and dozens of other towns were laid out—just waiting for the lots to be sold.

But there were voices that warned that the real estate was being built on shifting sands. The national business magazine *Forbes* warned that the land sales bore no relationship to the value of the land; prices were going up only because the buyers thought they could find someone with even more money.

The boom caused huge logistical problems. The three major railroads—Florida East Coast, Atlantic Coast Line, and Seaboard Air Line—were so overwhelmed with the freight heading south that they placed an embargo on everything but essentials. That meant building supplies to keep the boom going could not get through.

Potential lot buyers were told there was no way of knowing when their house could be built. The Florida East Coast Railway responded by borrowing as much as possible to build a second track. When the bust came, the railroad went into bankruptcy.

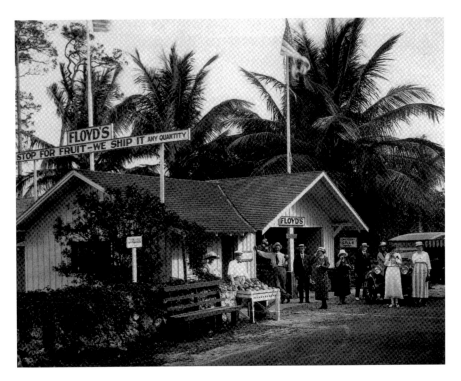

As the highway system brought tourists into Florida, roadside fruit stands were everywhere. This stand opened in 1922 and was the first in Miami. *Florida Archives Photographic Collection.*

Shipments were also delayed when the *Prinz Valdemar* sank in the mouth of the harbor and blocked access. Those builders who could not ship by railroad found they had lost the only alternative.

The delays caused builders to lay off construction workers, and that further slowed the economy. Many who wanted to build homes simply gave up.

28

FLORIDA WRITERS

By the time the Jamestown settlers and the Pilgrims arrived in North America, Florida writers had already produced a small library of books, poems and articles. For over five hundred years, Florida writers have found inspiration, a perfect setting or just a great place to write in the state's environs.

Thirteen-year-old Domingo Escalante de Fontaneda was sailing to Spain when he was shipwrecked along the Florida coast and spent seventeen years as a captive of the Indians. His dramatic 1575 retelling, *Fontaneda's Memoir*, became a bestseller and gave the world an early look at North American Indians.

Nicolas Le Challeux came with the ill-fated French in a 1565 expedition and survived to write the first poem about North America:

> *Who wants to go to Florida?*
> *Let him go where I have been,*
> *Returning gaunt and empty,*
> *Collapsing from weakness*
> *The only benefit I have brought back,*
> *Is one good white stick in my hand*
> *But I am safe and sound, not disheartened,*
> *Let's eat: I'm starving.*

Álvar Nuñez Cabeza de Vaca was part of an expedition that also ended in disaster, but he survived, walked from Florida to Mexico and wrote *The Relation* about his experiences. Most of it was factual, but Cabeza de Vaca

ZORA NEALE HURSTON

Zora Neale Hurston rose to fame as a writer in the 1930s and then faded into obscurity and poverty, though her popularity soared again after her death.

Her family moved to the African American community of Eatonville outside Orlando when she was a baby. Her mother died when she was thirteen, and she dropped out of school to help support her family. She went to work for a woman who encouraged her to read and gave her books.

She was able to go to high school in Maryland, and then she studied at Howard University and earned a two-year degree. A scholarship allowed her to complete her studies at Barnard College, where she was the only black student. She studied with legendary anthropologists Franz Boas and Margaret Mead.

She published her first story in an anthology called *The New Negro*, and in 1929, she returned to Florida, where she wrote *Mules and Men*. The book became a classic, but it was not published until 1935. Her other major novels were *Jonah's Gourd Vine*, *Their Eyes Were Watching God* and *Moses, Man of the Mountain*.

She found herself in the first rank of American authors, and her work was published in the *American Mercury* and the *Saturday Evening Post*. She wrote plays and newspaper stories, and during the Great Depression, she worked for the Works Progress Administration as a writer in Florida.

But she began to encounter difficult times. Critics objected to her use of African American dialect in her work. But there were greater problems ahead. The mother of a ten-year-old boy accused Hurston of molesting him, probably as a result of a personal feud. By the time Hurston was cleared of the charges—she was out of the country when the incident was supposed to have taken place—her reputation was seriously damaged.

She was also criticized for her conservative politics, criticizing the New Deal and backing the 1952 presidential campaign of Republican senator Robert A. Taft. She opposed the 1954 Supreme Court ruling *Brown v. Board of Education*, which ordered the integration of schools.

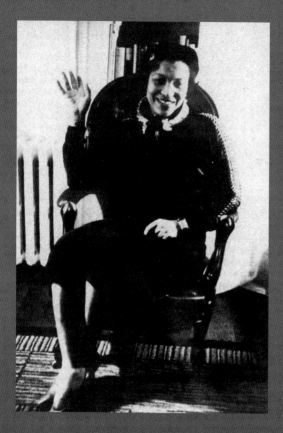

Zora Neale Hurston grew up in Eatonville and frequently wrote about Florida in her novels. *Florida Archives Photographic Collection.*

During the 1950s, she worked at the library at Patrick Air Force Base in Florida but was fired because she was "too well-educated." She took a job as a maid but was fired when her employers learned she was a famous writer and were embarrassed to have her working as their maid.

She went into a welfare home in Fort Pierce, where she died in 1960 and was buried in an unmarked pauper's grave. In 1975, writer Alice Walker revived interest in Hurston with a magazine article, and Hurston's books once again became widely available. Walker placed a tombstone on Hurston's grave.

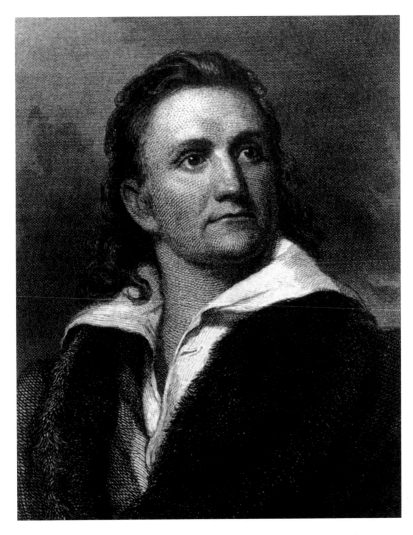

John Audubon came to Florida to paint birds and write about the state's beauty.
Florida Archives Photographic Collection.

also popularized the myth of the Seven Cities of Gold. His writings were translated to other languages and read throughout Europe.

These were just some of the hundreds of writers who have come to Florida.

Many of the early books were printed only in Spanish, and many readers in England and the British colonies were first introduced to Florida in the writings of Jonathan Dickinson, a leading Philadelphia Quaker. He was shipwrecked on Florida's east coast in 1669 while sailing home from

ERNEST HEMINGWAY

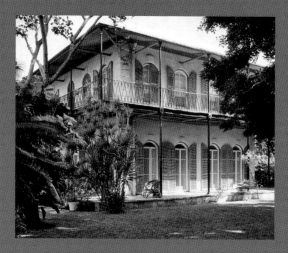

Ernest Hemingway bought this house in Key West in 1931. Built in 1851, it is now a museum. *Florida Archives Photographic Collection.*

When Ernest Hemingway arrived at the dock at Key West in 1928, he was already a famous writer. He had planned to stay a few days but ended up staying for years.

He stopped off on his way from Cuba to pick up a new car, but when he arrived, the car was not there yet. The Ford dealer apologized and offered Hemmingway an apartment until the car arrived. During the weeks he waited, he fell in love with the island and ended up buying the largest house on Key West.

When he first arrived, the island was isolated, but by 1938, a highway to the mainland had opened. Soon the tourists arrived, many of them coming to see the famous writer.

He told friends that he once hired a man to stand in front of his house and impersonate him for the tourists. They left thinking they had talked to the great man.

He wrote *To Have and Have Not*, which is not one of his better books, and the short story "The Snows of Kilimanjaro," one of his best.

As the population of Key West increased, Hemingway became disenchanted. He divorced his wife, Pauline, who got the Key West house, and Hemingway only returned to Key West a few times over the next two decades.

MARJORY STONEMAN DOUGLAS

Marjory Stoneman Douglas lived for over a century, enough time to see Miami rise from small village to giant city and to see the beautiful Everglades threatened by development and do something about it.

She was born in 1890, and one of her first memories was visiting Florida when she was four years old. She remembered picking an orange from a tree near the Tampa Bay Hotel. At the time, there were 400,000 people in Florida, and the settlement of Miami had just a few dozen people.

Douglas grew up in Massachusetts in a dysfunctional family. Her father and mother divorced, and her father headed for Miami to work for the *Miami Herald*. He hired Douglas as the society reporter in a town with almost no society—and only five thousand people.

She began her crusading with articles about Martin Tabert, a young man who was beaten to death in a prison labor camp. Her crusade led the legislature to reform the system of leasing convicts to lumber camps.

She left the newspaper and began writing for magazines such as the *Saturday Evening Post*. She was asked to write a book about the Miami River, but instead, she suggested she write one about the Everglades, which she called a "river of grass."

Developers wanted the Everglades drained to build more homes, the sugar industry wanted to dump waste there and the Army

Jamaica. His dramatic telling of the capture and cruel treatment of his little group—including his wife and infant daughter—by the Indians was reprinted dozens of times in the United States and England.

England's King George III named John Bartram the "Botanist for the Floridas," which brought him south in 1765. He brought his son, William, and the two of them gave the world a view of Florida's natural beauty. In Europe, the writers Coleridge and Wordsworth read William Bartram and used descriptions from his book in their writings.

John James Audubon came to Florida in 1831 to capture the territory's beautiful birds with his paintings. The Audubon Society was named for him. Another naturalist, John Muir, walked from Fernandina to Cedar

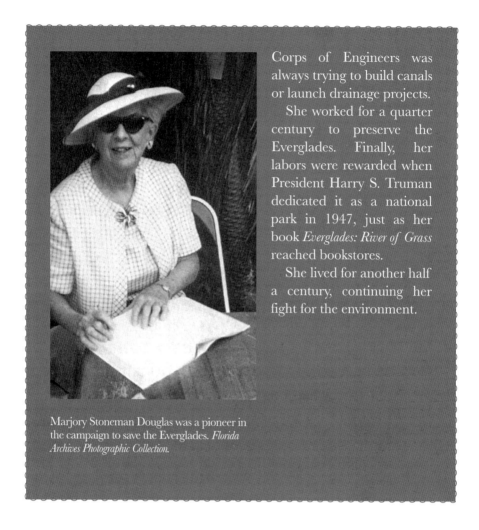

Corps of Engineers was always trying to build canals or launch drainage projects.

She worked for a quarter century to preserve the Everglades. Finally, her labors were rewarded when President Harry S. Truman dedicated it as a national park in 1947, just as her book *Everglades: River of Grass* reached bookstores.

She lived for another half a century, continuing her fight for the environment.

Marjory Stoneman Douglas was a pioneer in the campaign to save the Everglades. *Florida Archives Photographic Collection.*

Key and recorded his observations in his book *A Thousand Mile Walk to the Gulf.*

Some authors never set foot in Florida. Washington Irving met Florida's territorial governor William Duval and, impressed with Duval's exploits—largely overstated—wrote glowingly about him, turning the little-known official into a national figure. Irving, who is best known for "The Legend of Sleepy Hollow" and "Rip Van Winkle," at first called Duval "Ralph Ringwood" in an 1840 magazine article but in later articles identified him as Duval.

The poet John Greenleaf Whittier also never came to Florida, but one of his poems had significance throughout the country. When Captain

MARJORIE RAWLINGS

Marjorie Kennan Rawlings was born in Washington, D.C., where her father worked for the Patent Office. She began writing when she was just fourteen, contributing short stories to the *Washington Post*. After graduating from the University of Wisconsin, she took a job with the YWCA in New York and then became a newspaper journalist in Louisville.

She was working for the *Rochester Evening Journal* in 1928 when she and her husband moved to the backwoods of Cross Creek.

Marjorie Kinnan Rawlings came to Florida from New York in 1928 and settled in the community of Cross Creek. Her novel of Florida, *The Yearling*, won the Pulitzer Prize. *Florida Archives Photographic Collection.*

Her marriage was an unhappy one, and she divorced her unfaithful husband. She had already established herself as a talented newspaper writer and began contributing articles to

Jonathan Walker brought his ship to Pensacola, some slaves convinced him to take them to the British West Indies. His ship was captured, and Walker was arrested and returned to Pensacola. A federal judge ordered that the palm of his hand be branded with the letter *S* for "slave stealer."

Whittier's poem galvanized the nation:

Welcome home again, brave seaman! With thy thoughtful brow and gray,
And the old heroic spirit of our earlier, better day;
With that front of calm endurance, on whose steady nerve in vain
Pressed the iron of the prison, smote the fiery shafts of pain!

His poem went on to give the details of the case.

magazines. She used her neighbors as characters in her writing. Her first article, "Cracker Chidlings," appeared in *Scribner's Magazine* in 1931.

She received an amazing reaction to her first article, drawing praise from F. Scott Fitzgerald, Ernest Hemingway and Thomas Wolfe. Her first book was *South Moon Under*, which was a selection of the Book of the Month Club and a finalist for the Pulitzer Prize.

In 1938, she published her classic *The Yearling*, which became a bestseller, won the Pulitzer Prize and became a major motion picture. Her neighbors were surprised to see their lives captured in the book and themselves portrayed by actors in the movie. A few were angered, and one mother who recognized her son threatened to take a whip to Rawlings.

In 1940, Rawlings married Norton Baskin, who managed a hotel in St. Augustine. She became friends with Zora Neale Hurston—even though it was unusual for a white woman and a black woman to become friends in the 1930s—and Hurston was a guest in her home.

In 1953, Rawlings suffered a ruptured aneurysm and died the next day in a St. Augustine hospital.

Another writer had an even greater impact on the cause of antislavery, Harriett Beecher Stowe. Her book *Uncle Tom's Cabin* was read by millions of people, and the play version was seen by tens of thousands of others. It spurred the antislavery movement.

After the Civil War, Stowe moved to Florida, at first to help her son recover from alcoholism but later to promote the state for tourists and new residents. She wrote a series of articles promoting Florida that were published as a book titled *Palmetto Leaves*.

Poet Sidney Lanier was hired by the railroad to write about the wonders of Florida to draw tourists. Stephen Crane, who shot to fame with his book *The Red Badge of Courage*, nearly drowned in attempting to sail from Jacksonville to Havana to cover the revolution in Cuba. His ship sank, and Crane's story of his fight to survive, *The Open Boat*, became as famous as his first novel.

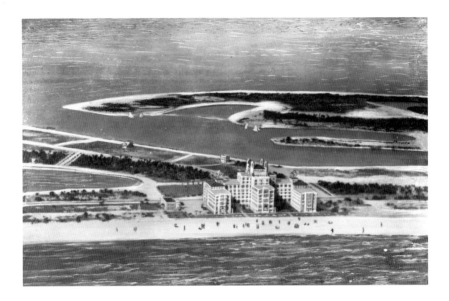

The Don Cesar Hotel in St. Petersburg Beach became a favorite of writer F. Scott Fitzgerald. It was there that he finished his novel *Tender Is the Night*, but it also held painful memories. While staying at the hotel, his wife, Zelda, had a mental breakdown and was hospitalized in Baltimore. *Florida Archives Photographic Collection.*

F. Scott Fitzgerald set two of his short stories in Florida and finished his novel *Tender Is the Night* while staying at his favorite hotel, the Don Cesar in St. Petersburg Beach.

Frederick Remington, the artist who captured the American West with his paintings and sculptures, was sent to Florida by *Harper's Weekly* to report on the Florida cowboys. He came away disappointed; the cowboys and the cows he found were inferior to those of the West.

Playwright Tennessee Williams bought a home on Key West, and poet Robert Frost became a regular before settling in Coral Gables.

Patrick Smith's, novel *A Land Remembered* captured Florida's history by telling the story of a single family.

Donn Pearce had the most unusual background. While working as a safecracker, he was arrested in 1949 and served two years in a Florida prison. He gained the inspiration for his novel *Cool Hand Luke*, which became a movie starring Paul Newman. The movie produced the classic line "What we've got here is failure to communicate."

John Rothchild captured the Florida of the boom years in *Up for Grabs* while Joan Didion's *Miami* reflected life in that city.

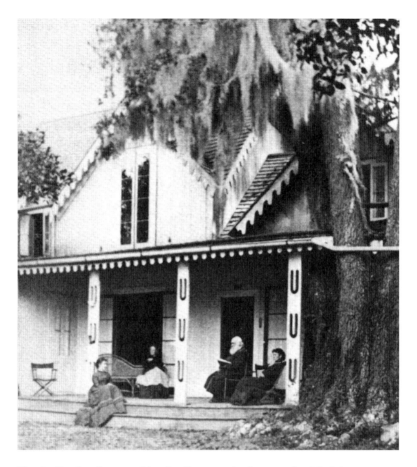

Harriet Beecher Stowe and her family sat on the front porch of their home on the St. Johns River near Jacksonville as steamboats passed. There was speculation that the boat companies paid her to come outside to allow passengers to gawk. *Florida Archives Photographic Collection.*

The *Miami Herald* has produced a series of bestselling writers, including Carl Hiaasen and Dave Barry. Hiaasen used Florida as the setting for a series of novels including *Tourist Season* and *Double Whammy*, and humorist Barry also found inspiration for his writings.

29

FLORIDA IN THE MOVIES

The film flickers, and the people are difficult to make out. There are children walking by, then a carriage, then seven hearses. It lasts just two minutes, but it is one of the first news films ever made. Thomas Edison made the movie in 1898 in Key West showing the funeral for seven men killed in the Spanish-American War.

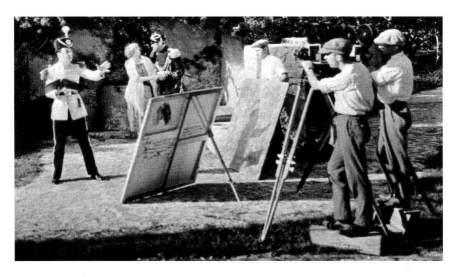

Early moviemakers such as these in 1925 in Coral Gables found that Florida was a perfect place to film. *Florida Archives Photographic Collection.*

TEN FLORIDA MOVIES

Hundreds of movies have been filmed in Florida since Thomas Edison first filmed a Key West funeral for victims of the sinking of the USS *Maine* in 1898. Here are some of the best known:

1. *Tarzan*. In the 1930s and 1940s, six Tarzan movies were filmed at Wakulla Springs and Silver Springs.
2. *Follow That Dream*. One of the movies Elvis Presley made was filmed in Ocala, Yankeetown and Crystal River.
3. *Parenthood*, starring Steve Martin was filmed in Orlando and Gainesville. Even though it was filmed in Florida, the movie is set in St. Louis. Careful viewers have spotted palm trees.
4. *Lethal Weapon 3* is not exactly a classic, but it is remembered in Florida because Orlando agreed to let its old city hall be blown up as part of the filming.
5. *Apollo 13*, starring Tom Hanks, was filmed around Cape Canaveral.
6. *Goldfinger* was filmed in Miami. It was the third of the James Bond movies. Another Bond movie, *License to Kill*, was filmed in the Florida Keys and then governor Bob Martinez even had a cameo as a security guard.
7. *Thunderball*, starring Sean Connery, was partially filmed in South Florida.
8. *The Bellboy*, starring Jerry Lewis, was filmed at the Fontainebleau Hotel in Miami Beach.
9. *Key Largo*, starring Humphrey Bogart, was filmed in 1948.
10. *Scarface*, starring Al Pacino as a drug dealer, was filmed in Miami. One of the scenes was filmed at the former Key Biscayne home of Richard Nixon.
11. *Citizen Kane* doesn't look as though it was partially filmed in Florida, but it was.

Other movies include *Ace Ventura: Pet Detective*, *Midnight Cowboy*, *Caddyshack*, *True Lies*, *Edward Scissorhands*, *Ironman 3* and *The Greatest Show on Earth*.

THE MOVIE STARS

Florida's first movie star was Oliver Hardy, who later achieved his greatest fame working with Stan Laurel in a series of Laurel and Hardy movies.

He was born in Georgia but moved to Jacksonville in 1913 to launch his movie career. He made more than fifty short movies in Jacksonville and then headed for New York.

The biggest star from Florida is Sidney Poitier, who was born in Miami while his parents were there to sell vegetables they grew on their farm in the Bahamas. He grew up in the Bahamas, but because of his birth, he had United States citizenship. When he was fifteen, he was sent to Miami to live with his brother. He worked as a dishwasher until he landed a spot with the American Negro Theater.

Burt Reynolds was born in Georgia but moved to Riviera Beach when he was eight years old. He was a standout football player at Palm Beach High School and earned a scholarship to Florida State University. His dream of a great football career was brought to an end by a game injury and a car accident. With football gone, he took up acting and won a state acting award, which included a scholarship in New York.

Johnny Depp was born in Kentucky, but his family moved many times before settling in Miramar. He dropped out of high school to join a band but quickly decided to return to school. His principal told him to follow his dream of being a famous musician. He and the band headed for Los Angeles, where he turned to acting.

Faye Dunaway was born in Bascom, a small town near the Alabama border. She studied at Florida State before earning her degree at the University of Florida.

Television star Delta Burke was born in Orlando and turned to acting after winning the Miss Florida title. She used her talent scholarship from the Miss America Organization to study acting in London.

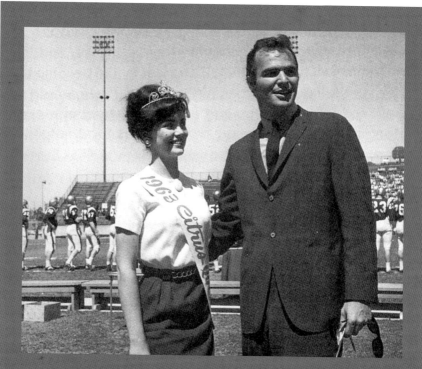

Former Florida State University football player Burt Reynolds poses with the 1963 Citrus Queen. *Florida Archives Photographic Collection.*

Other entertainers from Florida include Wesley Snipes, Orlando; Mandy Moore, Longwood; Mickey Rourke, Miami Beach; Angela Bassett, St. Petersburg; Cheryl Hines, Miami Beach; and Wayne Brady, Orlando.

One of the most famous movie lines was said by Thelma "Butterfly" McQueen, who was born in Tampa in 1911. A high school teacher suggested she try acting, and she became a dancer with several troops. Her first movie role was also her most memorable. Playing a maid in *Gone with the Wind*, she exclaims, "I don't know nothin' 'bout birthin' babies!"

For more than a century, the moviemakers have been coming to Florida. The movie industry began at Edison's studio in New Jersey. Edison held the patents to the movie camera and the projector and had an exclusive deal with Kodak to buy movie film. Anyone who wanted to make movies had to deal with Edison. Plus, it was often difficult to make movies in the winter with the cold weather and the early darkness. The moviemakers yearned to get away from Edison and the cold weather.

In 1908, a group traveled from New York to establish a movie studio in Jacksonville. Kalem Pictures—which was eventually acquired by Warner Brothers—produced the first feature in Florida, *A Florida Feud: Or, Love in the Everglades*, a critical look at backwoods Floridians. Next came *The Cracker's Bride*, another film that painted Floridians in a negative light.

Kalem found success, and soon there were nearly thirty movie studios in Jacksonville. What Jacksonville offered was realism for filmmakers. There were forests for jungle scenes, beaches for beauty and different types of houses for every movie requirement. Residents could see actors such as Theda Bara, Rudolph Valentino, Lionel and Ethel Barrymore and even Oliver Hardy, who later became half of Laurel and Hardy. In Jacksonville, Hardy made his first movie, *Bouncing Baby*, in which he played a very large baby.

In the first decade of the twentieth century, Jacksonville evolved into a major movie center, but problems were threatening the moviemakers. Jacksonville was a quiet, conservative town, and the moviemakers did not fit in. To finance their movies, some borrowed from local residents and never repaid the money. To attract crowds for a scene, they would pull a fire alarm and watch as people gathered. And they often filmed on Sunday, a day most people believed was reserved as a day of rest and prayer.

The end of moviemaking in Jacksonville came in 1917, when Jacksonville voters made their feelings very clear. Mayor J.E.T. Bowden was a major supporter of the movie industry while his opponent John Martin was a reformer who promised to reign in the excesses of the moviemakers. Martin won, and the moviemakers headed to California, where they had already begun making movies.

There was one exception, Richard Norman, who established Norman Studios to make movies with African American casts aimed at segregated audiences. He produced six major movies and hundreds of short films. His best-known film was *The Bull-Dogger*, starring Bill Pickett. With the advent of movies with sound, Norman was forced out of business, unable to afford the expensive equipment.

In 1938, the Fleischer brothers moved to Miami to produce their cartoons, which often rivaled Walt Disney's work in popularity. The Fleischer brother cartoons included Popeye, Betty Boop and the first Superman cartoons. But internal problems led the brothers to lose control of their studio, and it moved to New York after just a few years in Miami.

The opening of the Orlando attractions Disney–MGM Studios and Universal Studios Florida led many to believe that a new era was about to begin. The phrase "Hollywood East" was widely used. But the promise never became a reality, although many major movies continue to be filmed in the state.

The state has also been the backdrop for many television programs, including *Sea Hunt* in the early days of television, *Flipper* in the 1960s and *Miami Vice*, which is given credit for helping the revitalization of Miami Beach.

30

THE GREAT DEPRESSION

For the rest of the nation, the Great Depression is traced to a single day—October 29, 1929, when the stock market crashed. But in Florida, the Depression began in 1926, with the collapse of land prices. As one Floridian said, "We ran out of suckers to sell to, and started selling to ourselves."

But it wasn't just the people who bought land who saw their investment vanish. In fact, they were among the luckiest in the bust. Most put down a small down payment, made small monthly payments and could simply walk away from their investment while the cities and counties that had bet on the boom could not walk away. They had borrowed heavily—too heavily—and now were unable to pay.

St. Petersburg had the highest debt per capita in the nation, and Key West was a close second. The cities and counties had borrowed to build roads, schools and sewers and to beef up police and fire departments. They had bet on rising property taxes to pay the bills. The thousands of binder boys went first, fleeing the state. One St. Petersburg real estate company owner helped his binder boys leave in a very strange way. He contracted with local funeral homes to have them accompany the bodies of northern retirees on the journey back to their hometowns. They got a free ticket, and he got one less employee looking for a paycheck.

Land prices were already declining in 1926 when a terrible hurricane struck. The storm moved up the Atlantic along the Florida coast with 140-mile-per-hour winds and then suddenly turned west at Palm Beach and headed for Lake Okeechobee. It struck in the middle of the night, and most

AIRLINES

In 1913, there were two ways to get from St. Petersburg to Tampa, a twelve-hour trip by train or a long trip by boat across Tampa Bay. A businessman, P.E. Fansler, had an idea to create an airline to take passengers between the two cities. He purchased two seaplanes and hired pilot Tony Janus, and the world's first airline was born.

The first flight was on New Year's Day 1914. Three thousand people turned up on the St. Petersburg side of the bay to watch it take off. Mayor A.C. Phiel paid $400 for the first ticket, though fares were usually a modest $10 for a round trip. The plane held two passengers for the thirty-minute flight. The airline only lasted three months, and Janus died during World War I.

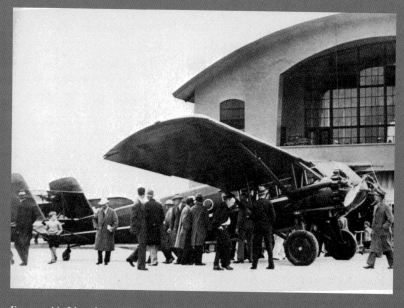

Eastern Air Lines began flying in 1926 and, five years later, started the Miami to New York run that brought millions of visitors to South Florida. *Florida Archives Photographic Collection.*

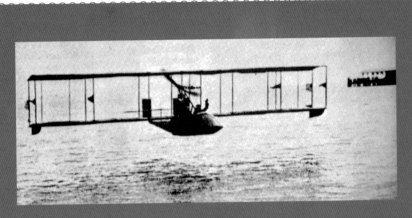

In 1914, the first commercial airline service in the United States began with a flight between St. Petersburg and Tampa, but the company lasted just a few months. *Florida Archives Photographic Collection.*

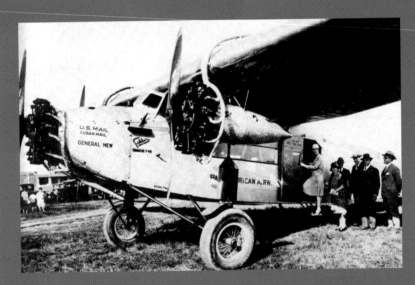

Pan American Airways began with flights between Key West and Havana in 1927. *Florida Archives Photographic Collection.*

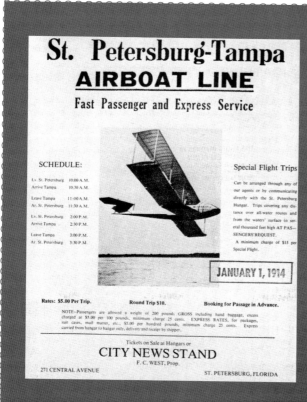

Tony Janus launched the first commercial airline service in 1914 with a short flight between St. Petersburg and Tampa. *Florida Archives Photographic Collection.*

During World War I, the importance of the airplane increased as the warring nations saw its power.

Three national airlines are linked to Florida. Pan American World Airways began flying between Key West and Havana in 1928 and became the world's leading airline. National Airlines got its start in 1934 in St. Petersburg with flights to other Florida cities. Eventually, it flew throughout the world before merging with Pan Am in 1980.

Eastern Airlines began flying in 1926 as Florida Airways in Jacksonville and later moved its headquarters to Miami. The airline failed in 1991.

TIMELINE 1920-1962

1920–26: The Florida land boom drives up property values and draws thousands of new residents.

1926: One of history's worst hurricanes hits South Florida.

1928: Tamiami Trail from Miami to the Gulf Coast opens, helping develop Southwest Florida. The first international flight from the United States takes place between Key West and Havana.

1930: Eastern Airlines launches Miami to New York air service.

1935: After being heavily damaged in a hurricane, the Overseas Railroad is turned into a highway between the mainland and Key West.

1941–45: Florida is a major training ground for hundreds of thousands of soldiers and sailors during World War II.

1950: Florida becomes the twentieth-largest state; first American rocket launched from Cape Canaveral.

1955: Florida Turnpike authorized.

1959: Cuban exiles begin arriving in Miami following Fidel Castro's rise to power.

1961: First American-manned space travel from Cape Canaveral.

1962: Cuban missile crisis.

people were asleep and had no warning. The true picture of destruction will never be known; state officials worried that news of the story would further dampen land sales and downplayed the damage to the nation's newspapers.

At least thirteen thousand homes were destroyed. Hundreds died—their bodies burned and buried to prevent disease, although critics of the state government said the bodies were disposed of quickly to prevent negative publicity. Around Lake Okeechobee, most of the dead were migrant workers whose shacks provided no protection against the wave of water.

The land boom was over, but the citrus industry remained strong. Then, in 1929, a grapefruit tree in Orlando was found to have the Mediterranean fruit fly, which decimated the citrus industry. Quarantines were placed on all citrus groves, and fruit shipments were banned. The National Guard was called out to patrol roads to prevent shipping oranges. Citrus production declined by 50 percent as half a million boxes of fruit were destroyed. Floridians who thought they could depend on the citrus industry to carry

FRANKLIN ROOSEVELT

Franklin D. Roosevelt was elected president in a landslide in 1932, and his inauguration was set for March 4, 1933. Before he took the oath of office, he came to Florida to cruise on the yacht of Vincent Astor. After a week on the yacht, Roosevelt docked in Miami, where he had agreed to make a public appearance in Bayfront Park before heading for Washington.

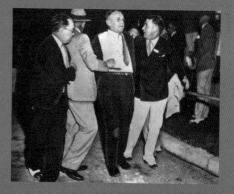

President-elect Franklin Roosevelt survived an assassination attempt in Miami, but one of the bullets mortally wounded Chicago mayor Anton Cermack (pictured). With help, he walked to a car for the journey to the hospital, where he died. The blood can be seen on his shirt near his waist. *Florida Archives Photographic Collection.*

The park is located in downtown Miami, and a large crowd gathered. Rather than have Roosevelt leave his car, get in his wheelchair and be taken to the stage, it was decided to let him speak from the back of the convertible he was riding in.

In the crowd was Chicago mayor Anton Cermak, who was vacationing in Miami and hoped to have a word with the incoming president. Cermak made his way to Roosevelt's car as the president-elect began his brief remarks.

As Roosevelt spoke, Guiseppe Zangara, an immigrant bricklayer, stepped onto a bench and began shooting at Roosevelt. Amazingly, he missed Roosevelt but hit five others, including Cermak, who later died.

Zangara was arrested and talked about a pain in his stomach but showed no remorse. Thirty-five days after the shooting, Zangra was executed in the state prison.

187

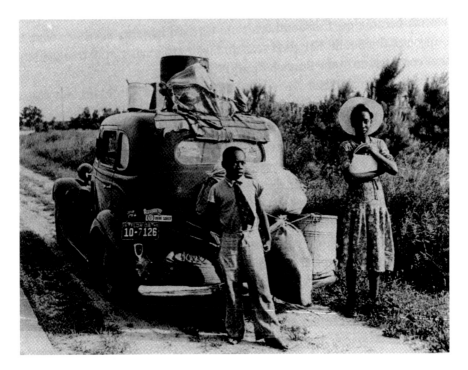

The Great Depression and World War II sent tens of thousands of African American families to the North, where there were better jobs and less discrimination. *Florida Archives Photographic Collection.*

them through found they were no better off than the landowners. Fortunately for Florida, two industries remained strong: cattle and phosphate.

It seemed things could not get much worse, but then the national Depression struck. To help pay the bills, Florida instituted a six-cent-per-gallon gasoline tax, which discouraged people from visiting the state. The rate was tied for highest in the nation in an era when gasoline cost just seventeen cents a gallon. Before the bust, two million tourists a year had flocked to Florida. With the economy in a tailspin, the number fell to one million.

Roosevelt's New Deal received a mixed reception in Florida. For many Floridians, the New Deal programs were a salvation, but business leaders did not like the intrusion of the federal government. Roosevelt's legislation to help labor unions angered the business community, and the sense among many white Floridians was that he was trying to aid African Americans.

31

WORLD WAR II

When Henry Flagler and his wealthy friends began coming to Florida in the 1880s, they stayed for weeks, even months, bringing with them trunks packed with clothing from the casual to formal—they were ready for any occasion. They brought servants to cater to their every need and remained for what became known as "the season." It was the period when the cold weather in the North was unbearable, and Florida was a wonderful alternative.

For decades, "the season" began on the first Sunday in December, and hotel and restaurant operators looked forward to the day. The Great Depression had decimated tourism, and the 1930s saw a slow climb back. In November 1941, the hotel keepers in Miami hoped that the coming season would be the best since the boom years of the 1920s.

When readers of the *Miami Herald* picked up their paper that December morning, they saw a story predicting better times. As they sat down to read their papers, five thousand miles away, their futures were changing; the hotels soon saw record occupancy rates, although not with the visitors they anticipated.

Japan attacked Pearl Harbor on December 7. It was afternoon in Miami when word of the attack first came over the radio. The war changed Florida dramatically, taking it from the smallest state in the South to one of the largest in the nation. On the eve of the war, it had 1.9 million residents, behind South Carolina and Arkansas. The largest city in the state was Jacksonville with 173,000 people. Cities that would one day have large populations were still small: Boca Raton had 723 residents, Sarasota's population was 11,000 and Orlando had 37,000.

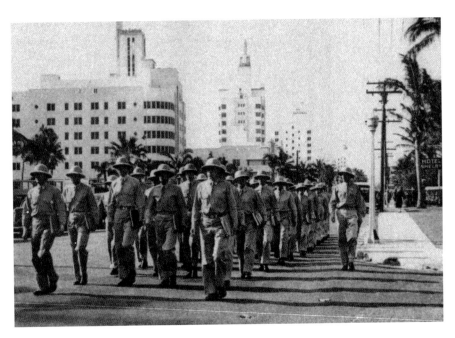

Soldiers marching through the streets of Miami became a common site as hundreds of thousands came to train and fill the town's hotel rooms. *Florida Archives Photographic Collection.*

In a small way, the war had already come to Florida. Six months before the attack on Pearl Harbor, President Franklin Roosevelt gave permission for British pilots to train in Florida. Britain could hardly train its pilots in England, where the Germans controlled the skies. Florida was selected because the weather made year-round training possible, and isolated areas meant clear skies.

Most existing flight schools were already packed with Americans, and the United States agreed to make some small airfields available to the British. One field was the Carlstrom Field in Arcadia, which had been abandoned fifteen years earlier, and the government sold the property for $500. The British also trained at Clewiston. In all, some 1,500 British pilots trained, and 25 did not return home, dying during training. They were buried in a separate section of the Arcadia cemetery.

Although the war began in Hawaii, it quickly came to Florida. Freighters carried oil along a predictable path from Texas, through the Gulf of Mexico, around Miami and up the East Coast along the Gulf Stream. It had been a route for half a millennia and was used by thousands of ships. In January 1942—the war was only a few weeks old—the Germans launched Operation

Drumbeat. Their submarines sat off the coast and waited for the tankers to pass by, backlit by cities such as Vero Beach and Daytona Beach, and picked them off like so many targets in a shooting gallery. In one ten-day period, ten ships went down from Fort Pierce to Boca Raton. In one of the worst attacks, the SS *Gulfamerica* was on its maiden voyage when it was attacked off Jacksonville Beach. The town was not observing the blackout. Nineteen men went down with the ship, and more than 100,000 barrels of oil coated the ocean surface. A year later, a blimp was shot down off Key West by a German submarine—the only blimp downed by submarine fire.

Along the coast, hospitals became adept at treating burn victims, some of whom washed up on shore, often covered with oil.

In, all twenty-four ships were sunk by the Nazis. One of the first acts of American involvement was to build PT (patrol torpedo) boats to attack the submarines.

A quarter of a million Floridians volunteered or were drafted into the military, and more than three thousand did not come home. An equal number suffered wounds. It means that one out of every eight residents served in the war. In Groveland, Mr. and Mrs. Robert Cockman sent eight sons off to serve their country, and all except Tommy came home. Two million Americans from throughout the nation came to train in Florida. Two future presidents trained in Florida: John F. Kennedy at the Submarine Chase Training Center in Miami and George H.W. Bush at the Fort Lauderdale Naval Air Station.

Colin Kelly of Madison was one of the war's first heroes. Three days after Pearl Harbor, his plane was shot down after his bombs hit the Japanese cruiser *Natori*. Kelly stayed at the controls while his crew parachuted to safety. In San Francisco, Japan Street underwent a name change to Colin P. Kelly Jr. Street. There were more streets named for him in Ohio, South Carolina and New Jersey.

In Washington, President Franklin Roosevelt wrote a letter to a future president asking that Kelly's young son receive a presidential appointment to West Point when he was old enough. In 1956, President Dwight Eisenhower honored the request, and Colin P. Kelly III went on to a military career and then to divinity school.

Alexander Nininger of Fort Lauderdale was the first recipient of the Congressional Medal of Honor during World War II, giving his life for his country in the Philippines. Sergeant Ernest Thomas of Monticello led the patrol that placed the first American flag atop Mount Suribachi on Iwo Jima. The war ended days after Lieutenant Commander Paul Tibbets dropped the atomic bomb on the city of Hiroshima. The plane was named the *Enola*

Gay, for his mother, who learned of the bombing at her home on Twelfth Avenue in Miami.

✴ Camp Blanding, a $700,000 camp for the Florida National Guard, grew so much that it would have been the state's fourth-largest city. It grew to 180,000 acres, and fifty-five thousand soldiers were stationed there, including wounded soldiers brought home from the African front and German prisoners of war. In all, there were 172 military installations in Florida, up from 8 in 1940. There were 40 air bases. One out of every seven soldiers in the United States military trained in Florida. Florida not only offered a grand climate, it featured perfect training facilities. Thousands of miles of coastline were available for practicing amphibious landings, and the swampy jungles prepared soldiers for fighting on Pacific islands.

The bases were hastily constructed, and the accommodations were often lacking. General Omar Bradley later wrote of one camp along the panhandle coast: "Camp Gordon Johnson was the most miserable Army installation I had seen…The man who selected that site should have been court-martialed for stupidity." At the navy's base in Fort Pierce, an inspection found that the only fit accommodations were in the base brig. Meanwhile, thousands of soldiers had first-class hotel rooms in Miami.

Miami's hotels were taken over by the military to house soldiers undergoing training. There, seventy thousand hotel rooms became a barracks for men and women from every branch of the service. The luxurious Breakers in Palm Beach, the Biltmore in Coral Gables and the Don Cesar in St. Petersburg Beach all housed soldiers.

Key West, limping along after going bankrupt during the Great Depression, underwent an amazing revival. The population went from thirteen thousand in 1940 to forty-five thousand five years later.

Miami's population soared from 173,000 to 325,000 at the height of the military training.

Tampa saw its cigar industry severely damaged by the Great Depression, but the construction projects at MacDill Air Field and two large shipbuilding companies hired thousands of workers at high wages. Locals joked that the Sunshine State might become the Steel State and that the peninsula would sink under the weight of the bases.

The boom created an unprecedented demand for jobs, and women took thousands of jobs previously held by men.

Florida was the setting for one of the war's strangest chapters. In 1942, four Nazi saboteurs came ashore from a German submarine near Ponte Vedra Beach. Four other saboteurs landed on New York's Long Island.

Their assignment was to bomb power plants and create havoc. One of the eight had second thoughts and went to the FBI. Six were executed, and two were given prison terms.

The United States began fighting in North Africa, and the Americans faced a problem—what to do with captured German soldiers. The solution was to bring them back to the United States. It was easy to set up prisoner of war camps in Florida—they did not require heat—and nearly two dozen camps were established for ten thousand prisoners. Many took menial jobs, picking oranges or vegetables.

African American soldiers were training in the Jim Crow South. They actually moved down a notch: white soldiers got the best train accommodations, then came Nazi prisoners of war and finally African Americans.

The state's citrus industry, which had suffered because of the Mediterranean fruit fly and the Great Depression, was reborn because of the demand by the military. Florida passed California to become the nation's leading orange grower.

After initially declining, tourism began to rebound. Florida cities urged visitors to come. "Like a soldier YOU need a civilian furlough," the Daytona Beach Chamber of Commerce proclaimed. Miami used the slogan "Rest faster here" to draw tourists. Attractions such as horseracing and dog racing were popular draws for both tourists and soldiers.

There were also constant reminders of the horrors of war. A large hospital was established at Camp Blanding, and some of the state's finest resort hotels—the Breakers in Palm Beach, the Biltmore of Coral Gables, the Don Cesar of St. Petersburg Beach and the Ponce De Leon Hotel of St Augustine—housed wounded soldiers.

Like the rest of the country, Florida endured wartime rationing. The government regulated 90 percent of all civilian goods. Rubber rationing came first, followed by gasoline and food. How much gasoline a person received depended on his or her job. Someone with an "A" sticker got four gallons a week. The result was that trains became jammed.

The end of the war saw wild celebrations from Miami to Pensacola and concerns about what it might mean to the Florida economy.

The war had forever changed Florida. In 1940, the population was 1,897,414, and by 1950, it was 2,771,305, an increase of 46 percent. Only California and Arizona had bigger percentage increases.

And it wasn't just that more people were moving in; it was where they were moving. In 1940, the state was almost evenly split between city and rural residents. In 1950, two-thirds of the residents lived in the cities, and the trend would continue.

32

MODERN TOURISM

The end of World War II brought a surge in tourism, which led to the creation of dozens of theme parks to draw the visitors—and their money. Historian Tracy Revels found that between 1946 and 1954, over thirty major attractions opened in Florida, and there were dozens of smaller ones. Many of the parks took advantage of what nature and the highway builders had given them. Park owners used local springs, creeks and wildlife and built everything from small roadside stands to elaborate parks to cater to the tourists.

A dense forest could be turned into a jungle-themed park, a natural spring could offer mermaids and fish and any body of water could promise that it was the real fountain of youth.

There were plenty of fish shows featuring porpoises and dolphins. One of the first was Marineland on the ocean south of St. Augustine. It began as a film set for moviemakers and opened as an attraction after the war. Others soon followed. There was the Aquartarium at St. Petersburg Beach, the Sea-Orama in Clearwater Beach, Ocean World in Fort Lauderdale, the Seaquarium in Miami and the Gulfarium in Fort Walton Beach.

Water was also the draw at Weeki Wachee Springs, which featured attractive women dancing, swimming and even eating beneath the water while crowds watched through a large glass window.

Wyoming might have been two thousand miles away, but cowboys became a staple in Florida parks. The biggest was Six Gun Territory in Ocala, but visitors had plenty of other choices: Pioneer City near St. Augustine, Fort Dodge outside Brooksville, Tombstone Territory in the panhandle and one

THE FIRST DISNEY

Walt Disney was not the first Disney to come to Florida. Elias Disney met Flora Call in Kansas, and when the Call family announced that they were moving to Florida in 1884, Elias and his father decided to go along. The rest of the Disney family soon followed.

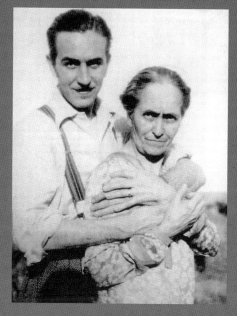

They settled north of Orlando. Elias and Flora's relationship flourished, and the couple was married in Daytona Beach in 1888. Elias operated the Halifax Hotel in Daytona, one of the first tourist hotels in the area. He also worked as a mailman and then purchased an eighty-acre orange grove near Paisley.

Walt Disney's parents, Flora and Elias, lived in the small community of Paisley. They married on New Year's Day 1888 in Daytona Beach. *Florida Archives Photographic Collection.*

A freeze put an end to his grove, and Elias Disney was left with a young son and no means to make a living. In 1889, he moved to Chicago and became a construction worker and then moved to Missouri, where Walt was born. As a child, Walt came to Florida to visit relatives but did not return until the 1960s, when he came to select Orlando as the site for his new attraction.

that was strangely named Petticoat Junction, the name of a 1960s television show, that was really a Wild West attraction.

As Revels found, many were simply started by individuals with a collection of something or an interest in something—whether the rest of

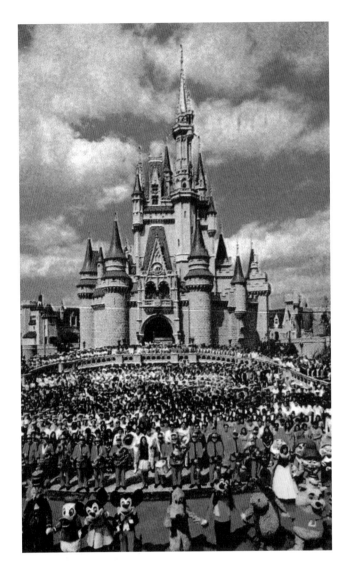

The original employees at Disney World pose in front of Cinderella's Castle during the 1971 opening. *Florida Archives Photographic Collection.*

the world cared about it or not. How else to explain the Cypress Knee Museum near Palmdale?

Some were of questionable taste and authenticity, such as the Tragedy in the U.S. History Museum in St. Augustine. It featured what it claimed were celebrity death cars and a collection of items that once belonged to Lee Harvey Oswald, the assassin of John Kennedy.

Sometimes they were little more than a roadside fruit stand with an alligator or two and a free glass of orange juice. Some tried to re-create

Africa in Florida, opening safari-themed parks. There was Jungle Larry's Safari in Naples, Africa USA outside Boca Raton and Lion Country Safari in Palm Beach County. Some, like Parrot Jungle, founded in 1936, and Lion Country Safari adapted and survived. Others found that the real estate values far outweighed the money they could pry from tourists. But most found that they could not compete as the traffic moved from two lane roads to the interstate, and the visitors wanted to see more than a woman swimming underwater.

Busch Gardens in Tampa started as a Budweiser brewery and became the nation's twelfth-largest theme park. In 1959, the brewery began offering tours and giving away beer samples, primarily to promote its beer. A few birds were added, and there was a "ride" called Stairway to the Stars, which was an escalator that took visitors to the roof of the brewery. At first it was all free. In 1965, an African-themed animal park was added, and the park started to charge an admission fee. As rides were added, there were extra fees. The park became known for its exciting roller coaster rides.

From the time Disneyland opened in Anaheim, California, in 1955, Walt Disney began to think about opening a second attraction in the east. A survey showed that just 2 percent of the visitors to Disneyland came from east of the Mississippi River.

He began his search in St. Louis, and for a time, it looked as though some sort of indoor Disney attraction might open there. But Disney lost interest in St. Louis and began looking at other sites. He considered Niagara Falls, then one of the most popular tourist destinations in the country, but realized it could only be open a few months because of the cold weather.

He considered a site outside New York but was worried that the big city would provide too much competition and the weather would limit the months it could be open. He also considered a site outside Washington, D.C., and near West Palm Beach.

Eventually, he turned to an area he knew all too well, Central Florida. He had come as a child and grew up hearing stories about the region.

Secretly, Disney began buying twenty-seven thousand acres. He worked through multiple layers of real estate agents so that no one knew who was buying the land. Soon there were rumors about who might be buying all that property. Some thought it was McDonnell Aircraft; others predicted Hughes Tool or the Ford Motor Company.

Emily Bavar, a reporter for the *Orlando Morning Sentinel*, went to California for a media event at Disneyland, and the reporters met with Disney. Bavar asked if he was the one buying the land. Disney said no. But in his denial,

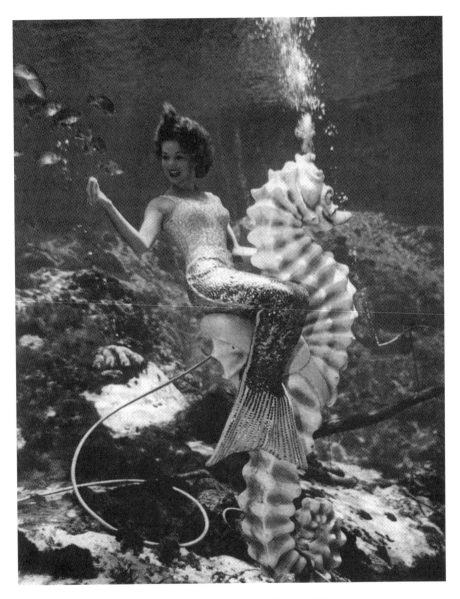

One of the largest tourist attractions in the era before Disney World was Weeki Wachee, which featured mermaids performing underwater in a natural spring. *Florida Archives Photographic Collection.*

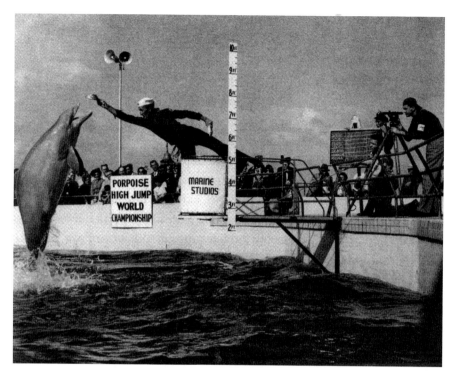

Marineland was one of the first theme parks in Florida. It began as a movie studio for filming underwater life. It opened in 1938 as Marine Studios and later became Marineland of Florida. *Florida Archives Photographic Collection.*

he mentioned specific facts about the area, and Bavar came away convinced that Disney was buying the land. The secret was out.

What was undecided was exactly what Disney was going to build. The initial announcement said it would cost $100 million, employ 4,400 people and include a "City of Tomorrow." His "city" would be a model for urban planning and feature real people as residents.

The October 1965 announcement came soon before Disney learned that he was dying from lung cancer. He died on December 15, 1966, still undecided exactly what he was going to build in Florida.

His brother, Roy, took over and decided that Disney World would be an amusement park. Walt's plan for a real city was shelved.

Walt Disney World opened on October 1, 1971, and the final cost was four times the original estimate. No one knew quite what to expect, but the reaction overwhelmed everyone, including Disney executives. Two months after it opened, fifty-six thousand visitors showed up on one day, and traffic was backed up for ten miles.

Orlando had just six thousand hotel rooms, and guests stayed as far away as Lakeland, Daytona Beach or Cocoa Beach. It set off a boon for nearby attractions. Cypress Gardens saw its visitor count increase by 38 percent, and Silver Springs drew 28 percent more tourists. Cypress Gardens owner Dick Pope had predicted that Disney would be good for his business, and for the moment, he appeared to be right.

Disney's Magic Kingdom was an experience that could be viewed in one or two days. Then tourists had the rest of the week to visit other attractions or head for the beach.

Within two years, SeaWorld opened in Orlando, its third park after California and Ohio. Hotel construction around Orlando soared, and everything went fine until the national energy crisis that began in late 1973. Florida tourism dropped by 15 percent in late 1973 and had dropped by 22 percent in early 1974.

Disney continued to think of expansion. In 1975, the company announced that EPCOT (Experimental Prototype Community of Tomorrow) would be build, a sort of permanent world's fair that many thought would draw many of the world's countries. It was clearly aimed at older visitors, but it also meant that visitors would now stay for an extra day or two, reducing the time they might have spent at other attractions.

EPCOT opened in 1982, and the park gave new life to the older park. Attendance at the Magic Kingdom, which had suffered for four years, shot up 81 percent.

In 1989, Disney added a third park, the Disney–MGM Studios, which became Disney Hollywood Studios in 2008. The attraction may have been more of an attempt to thwart the coming of Universal Studios. Since the opening of Disney, there was speculation that Universal Studios, which already had a theme park in California, would open an Orlando park. But Universal delayed the decision time after time. The idea first came up in 1982 but was put off until 1986, and the park finally opened in 1990, nearly two decades after Disney World.

By the time Universal was ready to act, a suitable plot of land was hard to find. Universal purchased a tract of land between downtown Orlando and Disney World. The original park featured rides and attractions based on movies and television series such as *Jaws*, *Murder She Wrote* and *The Flintstones*. In 1999, Universal opened an adjoining park, Islands of Adventure, which featured dramatic roller coasters and more exciting rides.

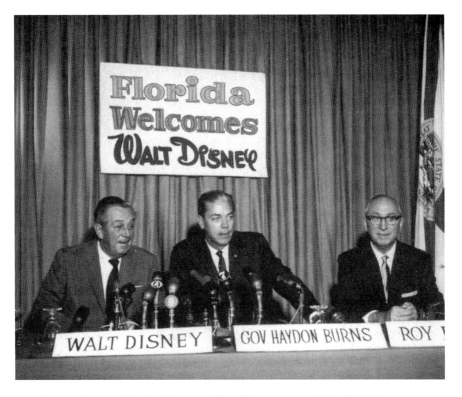

Walt Disney, Governor Haydon Burns and Roy Disney came to Orland in 1965 to announce plans for Disney World. *Florida Archives Photographic Collection.*

In 1995, Disney announced a fourth park, Animal Kingdom. It continued with a massive hotel-building program and made arrangements to transport tourists from Orlando's airport directly to Disney property. A guest could spend an entire vacation and never leave Disney.

The addition of all the new parks proved Dick Pope wrong. He thought Disney would be good for Cypress Gardens, but the opposite turned out to be true. All over the state, attractions that had been the staple of the tourist industry closed, unable to compete. In 1963, travel writers selected the Grand Canyon and Cypress Gardens as the top-two attractions in the United States. But with the coming of Disney and other Orlando-area attractions, Cypress Gardens began a slow death.

By 2000, seven of the nation's top-ten theme parks were in Florida, and Busch Gardens in Tampa just missed making the list.

33

FLORIDA POLITICS
1948–2014

Fuller Warren was the first governor to be born in the 1900s and represented a new voice in Florida politics. He was also the first governor to be a veteran of World War II—not World War I, as three previous governors had been.

He was forty-four years old when he won the governorship, and almost immediately, he ran into problems. Major business interests had put up the money for his campaign and demanded control of the state government, including making key appointments. There were also charges that some of his backers had ties to organized crime. During a federal investigation into illegal gambling in Florida, Warren refused to cooperate. He was the first governor to speak out against the Ku Klux Klan, and he pushed through an anti-mask law, even though he was a former member of the Klan. His political fate was sealed when he pushed through the state's first sales tax. When people made a purchase, merchants would say, "Don't forget the pennies for Fuller." He did plan for the Florida Turnpike and began to recruit Latin American tourists to come to Florida.

Warren was replaced by another progressive governor, Dan McCarty, who was elected in 1952 amid great promise. He took the oath of office on January 2, 1953, but suffered a major heart attack on February 25 and died on September 28.

At the time, Florida had no lieutenant governor, and McCarty was replaced by the president of the senate, Charley Johns. His title was "acting governor," and his term ended with a special election in 1954. Johns, a racist representing the special interests, lost in the primary to Leroy Collins, who is considered one of the best governors in Florida history.

Collins took over at the beginning of the modern civil rights movement. Months before he took office, the Supreme Court issued its *Brown v. Board of Education* decision, ordering schools to integrate. It outraged white southerners and led to calls for resistance. Collins was what was called a "moderate," which meant that while he was opposed to integration, he urged calm and respect for the law. He served six years as governor and then became president of the National Association of Broadcasters.

President Lyndon Johnson named him the first director of the Community Relations Service under the 1964 Civil Rights Act. Taking the post hurt him politically in Florida since it involved him with the civil rights movement. When Collins ran for the U.S. Senate in 1968, his opponent, Republican Ed Gurney, hired staffers—including a young George W. Bush—to distribute pictures of Collins with Dr. Martin Luther King Jr. as Gurney ran a racist campaign with promises to continue his opposition to all civil rights legislation, as he had done in the House of Representatives. Helped by Richard Nixon's presidential victory margin in Florida, Gurney defeated Collins. After his death, Collins was named Floridian of the Century.

Gurney served six undistinguished years and decided not to run for a second term after he became mired in a bribery scandal. He was indicted on seven counts of bribery and other charges, but after two trials, he was cleared. His attempt at a political comeback failed.

In 1954, William Cramer became the first Republican congressman elected from Florida since Reconstruction. Cramer's election was the beginning of the rebirth of the Republican Party in Florida—and the South. He represented the St. Petersburg area with its legions of conservative retirees from the North and military families stationed at nearby installations.

A decade later, Florida elected its first Republican governor since Reconstruction. In the 1964 election, the voters elected Jacksonville mayor Haydon Burns as governor. Burns served just two years as part of a Democratic idea to help the party. Dwight Eisenhower carried the state in 1952 and 1956, and Richard Nixon won in 1960. Democrats worried that a popular Republican presidential candidate might swamp state Democrats. As a result, they moved the gubernatorial election from the same year as presidential elections to off years.

Burns was a North Florida conservative who became known for his cronyism. He is also remembered as the governor who announced the coming of Walt Disney World to Florida. When his two-year term expired

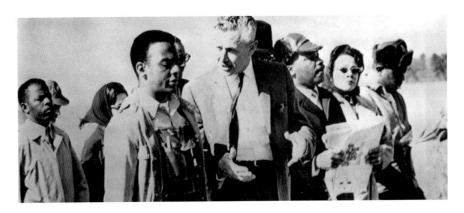

Political opponents used this picture against former governor Leroy Collins when he ran for the U.S. Senate in 1968. Sent by President Lyndon Johnson to monitor the civil rights march in Selma, Alabama, in 1965, Collins talked with Andrew Young, Dr. Martin Luther King Jr. and Coretta Scott King. Opponents claimed he was supporting integration by marching. *Florida Archives Photographic Collection.*

in 1966, he faced a primary challenge from Robert High from Miami. It was a classic battle: a North Florida conservative against a South Florida liberal. High won the primary as South Florida showed its political power. The party was left badly divided and could not unite around High. The Republicans nominated Claude Kirk, who became active in politics in 1960 by campaigning for Richard Nixon. Just two years after he was humiliated in a bid for the U.S. Senate, he won the governorship by a wide margin. He became the first Republican governor in Florida in nearly a century.

Kirk proved to be more of a show horse than a workhorse. He constantly sought publicity and hoped to be Richard Nixon's vice presidential running mate in 1968. Nixon passed on Kirk, and the voters grew tired of his antics.

In 1970, Kirk was defeated by Reubin Askew, who is considered one of the state's best governors. Kirk became a regular fixture in both state and national elections, failing at every level.

Askew was one of what became known as New South politicians who pushed a progressive agenda. He also became the first governor to serve two consecutive terms under a change in the constitution.

The biggest change during the 1960s and 1970s in Florida politics was in the legislature, where the Pork Chop Gang was on the way out. Florida's legislature was controlled by the smaller North Florida counties. A small panhandle county with a few thousand residents had one guaranteed seat, just as Dade County did with 100 times the population. Additional seats were based on population, but the small counties jammed into the panhandle gave that region extra clout.

The 15 percent of the people who lived north of Ocala controlled the legislature. The legislators from North Florida were called the Pork Chop Gang. They were all conservative Democrats whose platforms included strident racism.

The power behind the Pork Chop Gang was neither a legislator nor a governor but a businessman named Ed Ball. Ball was the son-in-law of Alfred I. duPont, a prominent member of the Delaware duPonts who sought self-exile in Florida, away from other members of his family. When duPont died, Ball took over control of the fortune. DuPont intended for his estate to help crippled children, but Ball had other ideas. He used the money to build a business and political empire, controlling over one million acres in North Florida through the St. Joe Paper Company and his Florida National Banks. Ball controlled the Pork Chop Gang, and the Pork Chop Gang controlled Florida.

In 1962, the U.S. Supreme Court issued its *Baker v. Carr* decision, also known as the "one man, one vote" ruling. The court held that unequal representation such as that held by the Pork Chop Gang was unconstitutional and ordered changes. Just as the state delayed the *Smith v. Allwright* decision, ordering the Democratic Party to allow blacks to register, and *Brown v. Board of Education*, which called for integration of schools, the Pork Chop Gang found ways to delay implementation of *Baker v. Carr*. A first try at implementing the changes was struck down by the courts. A 1967 special election produced a new legislature with the more populous counties gaining strength. The gains in the South Florida counties meant power for that region, and the election of substantial numbers of Republicans.

Askew was replaced by Bob Graham, whose family was in the cattle business in South Florida, and a major landowner. Graham pushed the legislature to pass bills protecting the environment, including major initiatives to save the state's rivers, coasts and the Everglades. He also approved the Wetlands Protection Act.

Bob Graham resigned as governor when he became U.S. senator, making his lieutenant governor, Wayne Mixson, governor for three days.

Graham was replaced as governor by Republican Bob Martinez, who served just one term. His popularity declined after he pushed through a services tax that was a sound idea to finance state operations. Unfortunately, the tax included newspapers, radio and television stations, and the criticism that followed cost him any chance of being reelected.

He also lost because the Democrats nominated former senator Lawton Chiles. When Chiles announced that he was going to leave the Senate after three terms, he planned to retire to his home in Lakeland and put politics behind him. Friends convinced him that he was the only candidate who could beat Martinez, and Chiles won in a landslide.

Four years later, Chiles faced a more formidable foe in Jeb Bush, the son of the president who had left office two years earlier. It seemed as though Bush would win easily. His father remained popular in Florida despite losing the presidency. Bush selected a weak running mate, Tom Feeney of Orlando, and Chiles proved to be a canny campaigner. He won by sixty-five thousand votes out of more than four million cast.

Four years later, Bush was back, running against a weaker opponent, Lieutenant Governor Buddy MacKay, and winning easily. On December 12, 1998, Chiles died unexpectedly, and MacKay became governor for three weeks.

Bush served two terms and was replaced by his attorney general, Charlie Crist. Four years later, Crist decided to run for the Senate, and it seemed clear to everyone that the Republicans would nominate Bill McCollum to replace him. McCollum served twenty years in the House of Representatives and gained a national reputation as the man who led the drive to impeach President Bill Clinton. He lost two tries for the U.S. Senate but then was elected state attorney general.

In 2010, he ran for the Republican gubernatorial nomination. To the surprise of everyone, Rick Scott, who had made a fortune in healthcare, jumped into the race, promising to push through and enforce tough immigration laws. He ran an excellent primary campaign, and McCollum seemed unprepared and lost. The Democrats nominated Alex Sink, who proved to be a poor candidate. Despite questions about Scott's past, he won by sixty thousand votes out of more than five million cast.

From the time Florida became a state until the 1970s, Florida voters automatically returned U.S. senators to office—just one was defeated during the 125-year stretch. At the end of the twentieth century, instability became the rule. In 1968, George Smathers decided not to run for reelection after three terms. He was a close friend of John F. Kennedy, and after Kennedy's assassination in 1963, Smathers lost his love of politics. He was replaced by Ed Gurney, who did not seek reelection. In 1970, the Republicans had a great chance to capture the state's other Senate seat only to see the chances evaporate as divisions within the party destroyed the opportunity.

Cramer was a natural nominee and had the support of President Richard Nixon. Governor Kirk and Senator Gurney split with Cramer and divided the party. The fight was over Harold Carswell, who President Nixon had nominated for the U.S. Supreme Court. Carswell was rejected by the Senate as being mediocre, and some Republicans thought he should run for the Senate. It turned into a political disaster. Cramer easily won the nomination, but the division destroyed Republican chances and opened the seat to a little-known Democrat named Lawton Chiles.

Chiles was a state senator from Lakeland who drew attention by walking a thousand miles from the panhandle to South Florida. As historian Mike Denham wrote, Chiles faced seemingly impossible odds in a race for the Democratic nomination against former Governor Farris Bryant. Chiles won in a runoff and then easily defeated Cramer.

Gurney's seat was taken by Richard Stone, who was Florida's secretary of state. Six years later, he faced a tough reelection battle. Stone faced the opposition of the AFL-CIO, and he had angered a number of powerful people in Florida. As he had six years earlier, he faced Bill Gunter in the primary, but this time, he lost. The divisions in the Democratic primary destroyed any chance they had of winning, and Republican Paula Hawkins of Winter Park won a narrow race. Hawkins proved to be unpredictable and a publicity seeker, and the voters turned her out after six years, handing her seat to outgoing governor Bob Graham.

Chiles and Graham each served three terms in the Senate. When Chiles retired in 1988, he was replaced by Republican Connie Mack, grandson of the baseball great, who narrowly defeated Buddy MacKay. Mack retired after two terms and was replaced by Democrat Bill Nelson.

When Graham retired after three terms, he was replaced by Mel Martínez, the first Cuban-American to serve in the Senate. He had come to the United States as a boy following the Cuban revolution. Martínez became disillusioned with the Senate and the political logjams and resigned after four years.

In 2010, the voters elected Marco Rubio, a Republican who was part of the Tea Party movement.

When Mel Martínez retired from the Senate after four years. Governor Charlie Christ appointed a replacement until the 2010 election. When he first announced for the Senate, Crist seemed to have the nomination sewn up. He did not figure on the rise of the Tea Party movement, which pushed the candidacy of little-known Marco Rubio. Once it became clear that Rubio would win the nomination, Crist ran as an independent. With three candidates in the race, Rubio won with less than 50 percent of the vote.

34

HURRICANES

From the time Ponce de León sailed along the coast in 1513, hurricanes have played a significant role in Florida history. The first recorded hurricane came in 1494 during Columbus's second voyage. In his ship's log, he records encountering a storm, writing, "Nothing but the service of God and the extension of the monarchy should induce him to repose himself to such dangers."

Another hurricane struck while his ships were anchored at Hispaniola—now Haiti and the Dominican Republic. Two ships sank, and only the *Niña* survived. By the time of his fourth voyage, he had seen enough hurricanes to know when one was approaching and warned the island's governor of the danger. The governor, Nicholas de Ovando, ignored the warnings and sent his fleet out. Some twenty ships and five hundred crew members were lost in addition to the gold the ships were carrying.

It is difficult to tell what the Spanish considered a violent storm and what was a true hurricane as we know it today. The first Spanish encounter with a hurricane in Florida may have come in 1546, when thirteen-year-old Domingo Escalante de Fontaneda survived a violent storm in the Florida Keys and was captured by the Indians.

In 1565, the first hurricane to play a role in Florida's history occurred when the French tried to drive the Spanish from St. Augustine. The French ships were wrecked, and the Spanish captured the French fort at present-day Jacksonville. The French aboard the ships washed up on shore south of St. Augustine, and most of them were executed.

One of several reasons the Spanish settled St. Augustine was to give their ships protection from hurricanes.

In all, hundreds of ships and thousands of people drowned as the Spanish tried to get their gold home. More importantly for Spain, thousands of pounds of gold went to the bottom.

One huge Spanish fleet sank off the coast of Cape Canaveral, although the Spanish were able to reclaim much of it. Still, enough remained of the gold that in 1970, the McLarty State Museum opened near Vero Beach with gold and artifacts from the expedition.

An 1843 storm destroyed the town of Port Leon on the Gulf coast of the panhandle. The residents voted not to rebuild the town, which had held promise of becoming a major port city.

Researchers believe that six of the most powerful hurricanes ever to strike the United States struck Florida. The most powerful was the 1935 Labor Day Hurricane; fourth on the list was Andrew in 1992; sixth was a 1919 strike in the Florida Keys, followed by the Okeechobee storm of 1928 and the Miami hurricane of 1926. Hurricane Donna, which roamed through Florida in the 1960s, it ranked ninth.

Hurricanes did not start getting names until 1950, and before that, storms considered to be memorable got names such as the "Great Hurricane," the "Big Hurricane" or the "Big Blow." There were so few possible names that several storms are known as the "Great Hurricane."

In 1844, a storm known as the Cuban hurricane caused substantial destruction in the keys. The local newspaper, the *Light of the Reef*, reported, "Houses, fences, trees, vessels, and almost everything in its course was leveled to the earth or borne off with frightful velocity."

In 1846, the first "Great Hurricane" tore through the Caribbean and destroyed 592 of the 600 homes in Key West. Even the two lighthouses were swept away and the occupants drowned.

By the 1800s, the Spanish authorities in Cuba had developed a somewhat reliable system for predicting hurricanes. It was years ahead of the Americans system, although the Americans usually ignored the Cuban warnings—something that would continue into the 1920s. Strangely, American shipping interests and insurance companies did heed the Cuban warnings and helped to finance the operations.

In 1870, President Ulysses S. Grant authorized the establishment of a weather-forecasting service under the U.S. Army Signal Corps. Twenty-four stations were set up to collect information and to warn of possible hurricanes. Eventually, there were more than one hundred

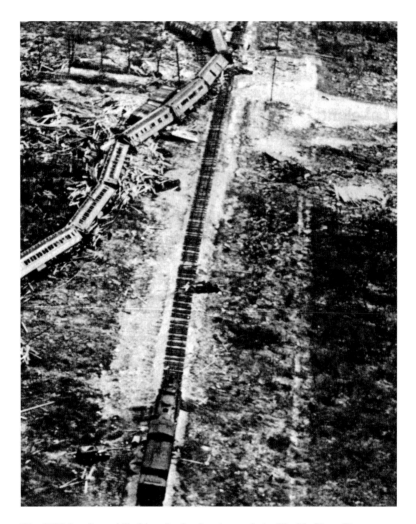

The 1935 hurricane killed hundreds when it struck the Florida Keys. Blown from the tracks, the rescue train could not reach the men. *Florida Archives Photographic Collection.*

stations, which depended on fragile telegraph lines that fell quickly in severe storms.

The service became the U.S. Weather Bureau. Florida was a weather outpost—storms often struck Florida first—and the forecast stations were able to warn points to the north of what was coming. Often, Florida had no warning.

There were other "Great Hurricanes" in the late 1800s and early 1900s, but one struck in 1919 that may really have been the "Great Hurricane." It passed over Key West, and the winds were so fierce—estimated at 150 miles per hour—that the instruments used to measure them were lost in the storm. The storm headed for Texas, and a total of 772 people were killed.

Until World War II, Florida was the least populated state in the South, and it was possible for storms to strike without doing significant damage or injury. The boom years of the 1920s changed that, and storms helped bring the Florida land boom to an end.

In 1926, the Florida land boom was beginning to falter, prices that seemed to have no limit began to decline and newspapers and magazines outside of Florida carried skeptical articles about the valuation. The one thing Florida did not need was more bad publicity.

The first hurricane of the 1926 season hit New Smyrna Beach with winds of 105 miles per hour, enough to rattle some of the recent arrivals.

The storm that entered the history books struck in September. On September 17, the *Miami Herald* contained a short story on the front page about an approaching storm without any sense of looming disaster. The brief story did not mention the word "hurricane."

Then, the storm struck with a fury never seen before in Miami. It brought the heaviest rain in Weather Bureau history. There was no evacuation—many thought that local leaders wanted to downplay the story to discourage a further decline in land prices and frighten perspective tourists—and the winds approached 140 miles per hour.

The instruments measuring rain were destroyed, but a guess is eight inches fell before the instruments did. Water was everywhere. Buildings were turned into kindling.

The new residents had never experienced a hurricane, and when the storm subsided, and the eye passed over the city, they thought the worst had passed and came outside to inspect the damage and perhaps seek safer quarters. Hotel guests left their rooms to go outside and walk in the knee-deep water. People jumped into their cars to flee Miami Beach.

It was a horrible trap. The eye passed, and the storm returned with even more viciousness than the first round. The remains of ships and buildings were flying everywhere, and hundreds of people were struck. The water that had been knee-deep after the first of the storm passed became six-feet deep, and people were swimming for their lives.

The storm moved inland and caused even more damage. In Moore Haven, the National Guard forced people to leave, even those who begged to search for missing loved ones. It crossed Florida, entered the Gulf of Mexico, picked up strength and struck Pensacola.

Hundreds were killed—the true toll will never be known—while one out of four structures in Miami suffered major damage. Hundreds of children became instant orphans.

Days earlier, the Florida East Coast Railway promoted special fares to travel to Miami. After the storm, it offered free fares to those wanted to leave.

The slow decline in land prices turned into panic selling. A piece of land that sold for $60,000 in 1925 went for $600 after the storm. Others simply abandoned their land, not even bothering to sell it.

The 1927 storm season was quiet, but 1928 was a repeat of 1926. There was a small storm in August that hit near Fort Pierce and caused flooding as it worked its way to Tallahassee and then into Georgia.

The worst came in September, almost exactly two years after the 1926 storm arrived. It is perhaps the second most deadly hurricane to strike the United States. It came inland at Palm Beach and dumped eighteen inches of rain and then headed for Lake Okeechobee, which offered the storm a fresh water supply. The lake was already high when the 150-mile-per-hour winds struck, bringing more water. Like many hurricanes, it came in total darkness, hitting shacks of mostly poor farm workers. Many were laborers brought from the Bahamas to work in the sugar fields.

The shacks were flimsy to begin with, built on cinder blocks off the ground. If the winds didn't knock them down, the floods carried them away. Hundreds sought safety in a packinghouse that became a coffin for 230 of them when it flooded. The waters carried one boy eight miles and then deposited him safely on land.

The area was so cut off from the world that it was two days before officials in Tallahassee began to learn the extent of the damage. Governor John Martin arrived and personally counted twenty-seven corpses.

The lesson Florida officials learned from the 1926 hurricane was that bad publicity hurts property values, and after the 1928 storm, they downplayed the destruction, delaying rescue operations.

Bodies piled up, and to prevent disease, they were burned, although critics later claimed it was to get rid of them before prying reporters arrived. In one pile there were sixty bodies, in another thirty. Some were buried in mass graves. Not all were accounted for, and for decades, farmers plowing their fields found skeletons left over from 1928.

While the 1935 Labor Day Hurricane did not claim as many lives as the 1928 hurricane, it carried its own tragedy. In the midst of the Great Depression, the government found work for some hapless World War I

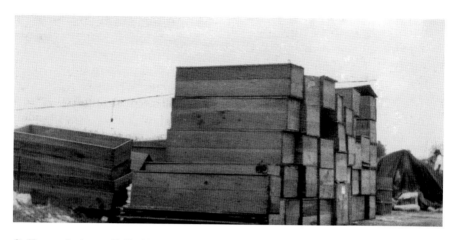

Coffins stacked up at Belle Glade to take care of the dead following the 1926 hurricane that decimated South Florida. *Florida Archives Photographic Collection.*

veterans in the Florida Keys. Hundreds of them lived in tents or shacks working on highway construction.

There were 684 men working for the Federal Emergency Relief Administration, and 300 of them escaped the barren area for a three-day holiday in Miami. With little warning, a small, intense hurricane bore down on the Lower and Upper Matecumbe Keys. The federal government failed to evacuate the men, waiting until the last minute to send a train to rescue them. The government delayed ordering the train, the Florida East Coast Railway delayed assembling the cars and the crew members delayed departing because of the holiday.

The winds were estimated at 150 to 200 miles an hour. More than four hundred men died needlessly. The rescue train was swept from the tracks. Writer Ernest Hemingway wrote a scathing magazine article blaming the Roosevelt administration for the failed rescue operation.

The next twenty-five years brought more hurricanes, but none nearly as deadly as those in 1935, 1928 and 1926.

By 1960, there were millions of Floridians who had never experienced a hurricane. Then, Donna struck. Like many before it, the storm started off the coast of Africa and first struck when it caused the crash of an airliner and the deaths of sixty-three passengers in Senegal.

It rose in intensity and, on September 3, became a Category 5 storm—the highest possible ranking. It was a Category 4 storm when it struck Marathon in the Florida Keys, destroying hundreds of homes and removing highways.

It moved along the west coast to Fort Myers and then took a turn to the east, moving up the middle of the state, over Orlando and reaching the Atlantic again at Ormond Beach.

Despite widespread destruction, the storm killed only four people. The damage was so great that Collier County moved its county seat from Everglades (now Everglades City) to Naples.

Florida avoided the worst storms until 1992, when Hurricane Andrew struck. It seemed as if the storm was aiming directly for Miami. For days, it followed a nearly straight line, growing to winds of 175 miles an hour and flattening nearly everything in its path.

Hurricane technology had progressed greatly since 1935, and residents had plenty of warning. Still, few had ever gone through a hurricane, and many failed to heed the warnings.

The storm struck at night—a small, compact storm—then moved west toward Naples. It didn't stay long, but the damage was everywhere. Homestead was all but destroyed with what remained looking more like a lumber camp than a city. There was damage from Miami to the keys. In all, 66,000 homes were destroyed, and over 100,000 others were damaged. The storm caused $25 billion in damage and killed forty-four people in Florida.

It also raised questions about construction standards and led to changes in building codes.

The 1995 season saw a wave of activity as two tropical storms and two hurricanes struck the state. The worst was Hurricane Opal, which struck near Pensacola, causing widespread flooding and damage as thousands of homes were destroyed.

The storms of 2004 impacted the majority of Florida residents, crisscrossing the state and causing widespread damage. Hurricane Charley was the worst to hit Florida in years, making landfall in Southwest Florida and leaving thousands homeless in Punta Gorda and Port Charlotte. The storm headed northeast, killing twenty-seven people and causing $14 billion in damage.

The state had not recovered from Charley when Hurricane Frances struck three weeks later between Fort Pierce and West Palm Beach and then moved slowly North through the middle of the state and into the panhandle, causing damage to areas already hit by Charley.

Two weeks later, Hurricane Ivan landed near the Alabama-Florida border and caused great damage. Hurricane Jeanne almost duplicated the path followed by Frances.

35

AIR CONDITIONING

If the world had listened to Dr. John Gorrie, air conditioning might have come a century earlier. Instead, he was dismissed as a fool and died in poverty.

In the 1830s, Gorrie worked in the U.S. Marine Hospital in the tiny town of Apalachicola, Florida. He thought that lowering the temperature would help his malaria and yellow fever patients. In the 1830s, Gorrie developed a crude system to cool rooms. He passed air over blocks of ice suspended from the ceiling. The cool air passed to the patients. At the time, ice had to be brought from far away lakes and was expensive, and Gorrie began to experiment with a machine to make ice. As Raymond Arsenault found in his history of southern air conditioning, Gorrie continued with his research even though his tests were mixed.

Gorrie's work led him to develop an ice-making machine, which he patented in 1851. It might be expected that the world would hail his invention, but he was met with opposition from the ice industry and scorn from journalists, including one who wrote, "A crank down in Florida thinks he can make ice as good as Almighty God." He spent all of his money trying to perfect his invention; then an investor died, and Gorrie was ruined.

Today, a statue of Gorrie stands in Statuary Hall in the U.S. Capitol. He is recognized as the inventor of air conditioning, but his work was forgotten at the time. He died in 1855.

Florida, and the rest of the world, would have to wait and continue to sweat.

In 1882, the electric fan was invented, replacing a steam-powered model that had been used to provide air to factories. Steam power was impractical

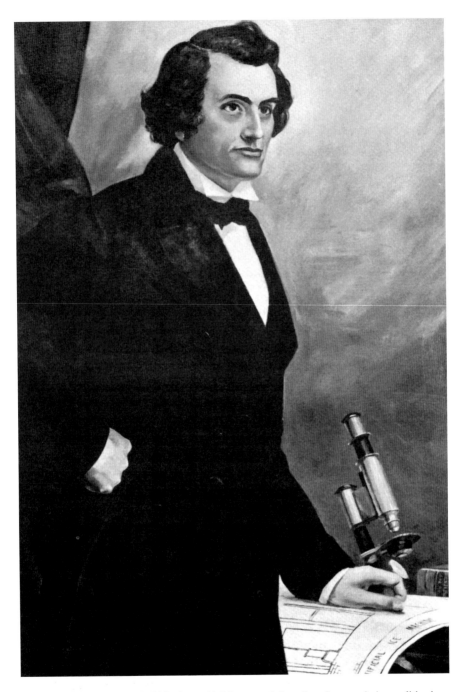

John Gorrie was far ahead of his time with his research in yellow fever and air conditioning. He died broke but received long-overdue recognition with a statue in the U.S. Capitol. *Florida Archives Photographic Collection.*

for homes. While the electric fan provided some minor relief, the real problem in Florida was the humidity, which made people and everything they wore wet with perspiration.

In 1902, twenty-five-year-old Willis Carrier came up with a system that cooled and removed humidity. By 1906, his system was being called "air-conditioning."

Like the steam-powered fans, the early air-conditioning systems were designed for large factories and then for hotels and movie theaters. In 1922, Carrier came up with a system to reduce the size of his air conditioner with an eye toward making it practical for smaller businesses.

As historian Raymond Arsenault found, the 1950s witnessed rapid improvements in air conditioning that changed Florida. As early as 1914, air conditioning in homes was available; however, the systems were large and expensive and drew few buyers.

In 1951, a small window air conditioner hit the market, and by 1955, nearly one in ten homes in the South could boast some type of air conditioning. By 1960, almost one out of five Florida homes had air conditioning, although the percentage was just 2 percent for the homes owned by African Americans. The number increased to 60 percent in 1970 and 84 percent in 1980.

Usually families started with a single window air conditioner and then added a second and perhaps a third unit before switching to a total-home system. Today, throughout Florida, it is possible to see homes where window air conditioners have been removed and replaced with wood or not-quite-matching cinder blocks.

Before air conditioning, houses were usually built off the ground and featured large windows and high ceilings to allow for the flow of air. After air conditioning, houses could be constructed more cheaply on a concrete slab. Hundreds of thousands of inexpensive cinderblock homes were erected throughout Florida, perfect for retirees and young couples on a budget.

It changed the quality of life. People were used to waking up in the middle of the night to change sheets wet from perspiration. A study in 1962 found that people were sleeping an hour longer at night during the summer, families were eating more hot meals and laundry and cleaning time was cut in half.

Along with the air-conditioned home came the air-conditioned car, and by 1973, eight out of ten cars sold in the South came equipped with air conditioning. It was possible in Florida to live a totally air-conditioned life, sleeping in an air-conditioned home, driving to work in an air-conditioned car, working in an air-conditioned office, shopping in air-conditioned stores and being entertained in air-conditioned theaters.

36

CIVIL RIGHTS IN FLORIDA

After Reconstruction ended in 1877, African Americans lost what little protection they had from the federal government. By 1890, only Jacksonville and Pensacola still had African American officials in elective office. They did not lose all their rights; they could still vote, primarily because their Republican votes were overwhelmed by Democratic votes. As the former Confederates regained the vote and as a new generation of white Democrats came along, the Republicans saw their majorities vanish. The Republican candidate for governor took 59 percent of the vote in 1868, 52 percent four years later, 49.8 percent in 1876 and 45 percent in 1880.

The 1880s saw a new threat to the men who controlled state government: the Populist Movement. Small farmers joined the National Farmers Alliance, and the national convention was held in Ocala in 1890 in a large barn. The farmers issued what became known as the Ocala Platform and called for the regulation of interstate railroads, expansion of silver money and direct election of senators. Eventually, all three would happen.

The Populists argued that if poor white farmers and poor black farmers came together, they could take control of government and pass whatever laws they chose. That thought struck fear among the wealthy class that controlled the state.

JAMES WELDON JOHNSON

James Weldon Johnson had the choice of going to Harvard University and becoming a doctor or teaching in his native Jacksonville in a school with few resources for African American students.

Johnson was born in Jacksonville in 1874, graduated from Atlanta University and then became president of Stanton School. When he arrived, the school was primarily vocational, aimed at preparing African Americans for menial jobs. Johnson added a number of academic subjects, including Spanish, algebra and physics.

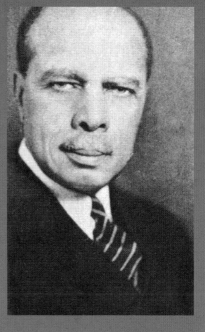

He founded a daily newspaper, which lasted just eight months, and became a lawyer—all while working at the school.

Jacksonville native James Weldon Johnson became an early civil rights leader. *Florida Archives Photographic Collection.*

He and his brother also began writing songs, including "Lift Every Voice and Sing," which became known as the African American National Anthem.

He later became consul to Venezuela and Nicaragua and wrote *The Autobiography of an Ex-Colored Man.*

He became executive secretary of the National Association for the Advancement of Colored People, the first African American to hold that post, and a decade later was named a professor at Fisk University. He was one of the nation's best-known African Americans when a train struck his car and killed him in 1938.

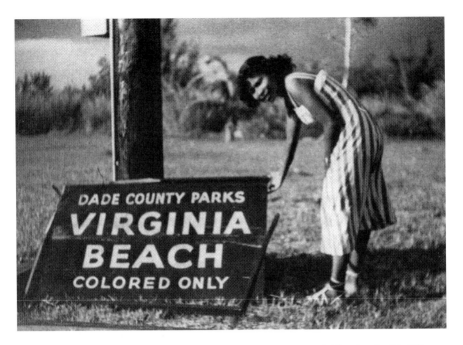

The state's Jim Crow laws required Florida's beaches to be segregated. The sign for this African American beach in Miami fell during a 1950 storm. *Florida Archives Photographic Collection.*

Florida and states throughout the South met the threat with legislation to separate the races and to deny rights to blacks. Between 1885 and 1889, legislation was passed to limit the rights of blacks.

The Florida legislature passed the poll tax, a fee to cast a ballot that effectively eliminated tens of thousands of voters, both white and black. There was also legislation to require literacy tests, and even those who could read and write often found that they were given questions that were impossible to answer, such as "How many bubbles are there in a bar of soap?" If somehow blacks made it through the maze of requirements, there were threats of violence and a voting procedure that made casting a ballot almost impossible. For illiterate whites, there was the grandfather clause, which held that if someone's grandfather could vote, then they could vote. The grandfathers of illiterate whites could vote while blacks whose grandfathers were illiterate slaves could not.

Florida was the first southern state to drop the poll tax, largely as a result of the work of state senator Ernest Graham, whose bold stand cost him white votes and possibly the governorship. Four decades after he failed in

THE RACE RIOTS

The 1920s brought massive changes in America. There was a rebirth of the Ku Klux Klan and racial violence. Florida saw more than its share of racial violence, particularly in three cities.

In Ocoee in 1920, Mose Norman and July Perry registered their fellow blacks to vote, drawing the attention and wrath of the Ku Klux Klan. When Norman and Perry went to the polls, they were turned away. When Norman returned, he was beaten and never heard from again. A mob went to the Perry's home and lynched him. In the rioting that followed, an unknown number of blacks died, including a pregnant woman. Many people believe the Klan attack was a plan by whites to seize their land, home and crops. All of the town's black residents fled, and it would be sixty years before African Americans returned to the town.

In Perry in 1922, Charles Wright, an escaped convict, and an accomplice were arrested and charged with the murder of a white schoolteacher. A mob of several thousand whites gathered and took Wright from the jail, tortured him and burned him to death. The rioting mob killed two more black men and burned the town's black school, as well as several black-owned homes and businesses.

In Rosewood, a small town west of Ocala, six African Americans and two whites were killed, and the town was destroyed. The small town had a primarily African American population with a stop on the Seaboard Air Line Railway. A white woman claimed a black man beat her, and local whites lynched a Rosewood resident in retaliation.

Several hundred whites gathered and began searching the countryside for more blacks. Nearly every building in Rosewood was burned. The survivors hid in nearby swamps and had to be evacuated. Law enforcement officials took no action, and the town was never rebuilt. Sixty years later, the survivors began telling their stories, and in 1993, the Florida legislature investigated and ordered compensation for the survivors. A movie starring Jon Voigt was made about the Rosewood incident.

his attempt to be governor, his son, Bob Graham, captured the office that eluded his father.

By 1900, the new laws had done their work. The Republican candidate for governor received just 17 percent of the vote. In some North Florida counties where blacks were in the majority, not a single vote was cast by an African American. This continued for another six decades.

The restrictions became known as the Jim Crow laws, named for a white minstrel who painted his face black with burnt cork and sang songs. There were separate train cars for blacks and whites; on the horse-drawn streetcars, blacks sat in the back and had to give up their seats if the car filled up. Everywhere there were separate entrances—for factories, for offices, even for the traveling circus that came to town. White nurses could not treat black patients, black barbers could not cut the hair of whites and, in the theaters, African Americans sat in the balcony.

A quarter of a million African Americans, 44 percent of the population, found themselves with no power or protection. By 1910, many blacks gave up hope of ever achieving anything approaching equality with whites and began leaving the state. Most blacks worked in menial jobs, picking oranges and vegetables or working the sugar industry in the desperately poor area around Lake Okeechobee. If women were not in the fields, they worked as maids or in laundries.

It became known as the Great Migration—tens of thousands of blacks heading north for jobs and the vote. It lasted until the end of World War II, and when it was over, the percentage of blacks in the state had been cut in half.

The goal of the Jim Crow laws was to control African Americans, to keep them picking oranges or vegetables and not striving for anything better.

Many of the blacks who remained left the old Cotton Belt of North Florida for the southern part of the state, where there were better-paying jobs in phosphate mining and the luxury hotels.

The U.S. Supreme Court gave support to the segregationists with the 1896 *Plessey v. Ferguson* decision, which approved the doctrine of separate but equal. While conditions were separate, they were far from equal. When whites were through with a train car, it was passed on to blacks, old school buildings and textbooks went to them, black schoolchildren could count on going to school much less than their white counterparts and their teachers were paid far less. In 1901, the average white teacher had thirty-nine pupils and the average black teacher had seventy-nine. In Gainesville, black teachers earned $562 in 1935 while their white counterparts made $970.

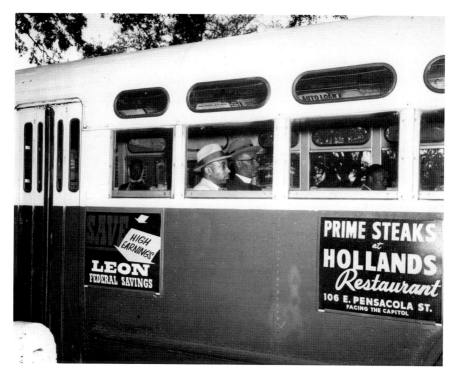

Reverend C.K. Steele (next to the window) and Reverend Dan Speed demonstrate to force busses in Tallahassee to treat African Americans equally. The demonstrations in 1956 were successful. Today, there is a statue of Steele in Tallahassee. *Florida Archives Photographic Collection.*

Beginning with World War II, things began to slowly change. For more than half a century, the Democratic Party had acted as though it were a private club, able to admit anyone it chose, and it only chose whites. In 1944, the Supreme Court in the *Smith v. Allwright* decision, the Democratic Party was ordered to allow blacks to register.

World War II sent thousands of Florida's African Americans to the North or to Europe, where there were no Jim Crow laws. They came home unwilling to return to the citrus groves and do the bidding of the whites.

The white resistance turned violent, with the Ku Klux Klan activity centered in the small town of Apopka, near Orlando. The Klan operated with impunity. The sheriff of Orange County, Dave Starr, was a member of the Klan, and in neighboring Lake County, the violent, racist Sheriff Willis McCall denied he was a member of the Klan, although he did attend the Klan meetings.

GROVELAND

In 1949, Norma Padgett told police she was attacked by four men. Her claim set off a string of events that led to two deaths, an attempt to murder a future Supreme Court justice and the murder of a civil rights leader.

Groveland was a small citrus town where black families owned land. Groveland blacks returning from World War II wanted more than a life in the orange groves, creating problems for the racist sheriff, Willis McCall, whose primary job was to use any means to keep blacks working in the fields.

Two former soldiers, Samuel Shepherd and Walter Irvin, were reportedly told bluntly by McCall to take off their uniforms and get to work in the fields.

Shortly after Padgett's claim, Shepherd, Irvin and two other African Americans were accused of kidnapping and raping her and assaulting her husband, Willie. One of the four, Ernest Thomas, was shot and killed by McCall as a posse tracked him down.

Led by the Ku Klux Klan from Apopka, some five to six hundred men swarmed over Groveland and set fire to black homes and shot into them. The Shepherd home was destroyed, and the black families fled. Governor Fuller Warren sent in the National Guard to restore peace

The violence began in the 1920s in small towns like Perry, Ocoee and Rosewood. From 1900 to 1930, some 140 black men and women were lynched in the state—the highest percentage based on population in the South. The records of the National Association for the Advancement of Colored People tell the story—the "crimes" included insulting a white woman, refusing to sell land and alleged murder or rape, all leading to execution without a trial.

In the 1940s, the tension exploded. Black leaders Harry T. Moore and C.K. Steele found their lives threatened, and the Apopka Klan killed Moore on Christmas Night 1951. The hate was not limited to blacks; in Miami, there were bombings at a synagogue. There was even an attempt by the Klan to kill future Supreme Court justice Thurgood Marshall in Lake County.

Shepherd, Irvin and Charles Greenlee were convicted despite clear evidence that they were framed and that they had been beaten by deputies. The judge refused to allow the defense to call as a witness the doctor who examined Padgett. One of the defense attorneys was future Supreme Court justice Thurgood Marshall, who was nearly killed by the Klan on a lonely country road. And Greenlee seemed to have to the best alibi—he was in jail in an adjoining county at the time the supposed attack took place.

Greenlee, a juvenile, was sentenced to life in prison while Shepherd and Irvin received the death penalty. They were transferred to the state prison in Starke to await execution. The U.S. Supreme Court overturned their convictions and ordered a new trial. McCall drove Shepherd and Irvin back to Lake County. He claimed that he stopped to change a tire and the two manacled men jumped him. He said he was forced to shoot them, killing Shepherd, and he thought killing Irvin. Irvin survived and said that McCall had murdered Shepherd and tried to kill him.

Irvin was retried and found guilty again. In 1955, Governor Leroy Collins commuted his sentence to life, and he was paroled in 1968. He died two years later. Greenlee was paroled in 1962.

The Federal Bureau of Investigation produced evidence that the three men had been tortured by McCall and evidence planted. U.S. attorney Herbert Phillips, a racist, refused to act.

In 1964, Dr. Martin Luther King Jr. brought his Southern Christian Leadership Conference to St. Augustine, and he would later say it was the only time he had truly been afraid for his life. A sit-in at the Woolworth lunch counter resulted in the arrest of sixteen people, including four children, who were sent to reform school. The fate of the children drew protests throughout the country, and the governor ordered them freed. Predictably, the Florida legislature blamed black Muslims from Jacksonville and "northern agitators" for the violence.

Klan nightriders responded to the demonstrations by terrorizing black neighborhoods and beating NAACP activists with chain clubs. The local sheriff arrested the victims for assaulting the Klansmen who carried out the violence. A cottage where King was supposed to stay went up in flames.

HARRY T. MOORE

On Christmas night 1951, a huge bomb exploded beneath a small, wooden house in Mims, Florida, killing Harry T. Moore and mortally injuring his wife. Moore became the first civil rights leader to be assassinated in the United States.

In 1934, he organized the Brevard County chapter of the National Association for the Advancement of Colored People. He was a shy and quiet man but was effective in signing up new members. He brought the first suit in Florida, challenging the low pay African American teachers received—often half of what white teachers were paid.

He lost his job as the principal of a black school because of his activities, and his wife was fired as a teacher. He organized the state NAACP and became the first NAACP state conference president in the country.

He formed the Progressive Voters League to increase voter registration. While the NAACP was nonpartisan, the PVL was dedicated to finding candidates who were the most supportive of blacks and backing them.

By 1950, Florida had the highest percentage of registered black voters in the South. The push for equality led to violent reactions as bombings swept the state and blacks were beaten and killed.

Moore became involved in the defense of the Groveland Four and helped bring future Supreme Court justice Thurgood Marshall into the court fight.

The NAACP grew increasingly uncomfortable with Moore's political involvement and forced him out. A months later, the bomb exploded beneath his home and nearly destroyed the small frame home. Moore died soon after arriving at the hospital, and his wife died a few days later. The FBI determined that the Apopka Ku Klux Klan was responsible for the murder only to find the federal government lacked the jurisdiction to take any action.

King was arrested, along with protesters who attempted to integrate the beach on Anastasia Island.

When protesters tried to integrate the swimming pool at the Monson Motor Lodge, the manager poured in gallons of pool chemicals to get them out. Police jumped into the pool to arrest them.

King urged rabbis to come to St. Augustine, and on June 18, there was a mass arrest of rabbis who had come from across the nation to join King.

The work of the civil rights pioneers paid off. In Moore's home county, Brevard, half of the African American voters were registered to vote by 1950.

In 1964, Congress passed the Civil Rights Act and followed it the next year later with the Voting Rights Act. Florida's two senators at the time, Spessard Holland and George Smathers, both voted against the civil rights legislation. In a two-month filibuster to prevent the Civil Rights Act from coming to a vote, Holland vowed, "We'll stand up and fight as long as we can."

In 1968, Joe Lang Kershaw was elected to the Florida House as the first black member since Reconstruction, and fourteen years later, Carrie Meek and Arnett Girardeau went to the state senate.

Progress was slow, and there was a major riot in Miami's Liberty City in 1980. As late as 1996, there was a race riot in St. Petersburg.

Joseph Hatchett, the son of a maid and a cotton picker, became the first African American on the Florida Supreme Court. In 1975, he was appointed by Governor Reubin Askew and reelected by the voters the following year. In 1990, Leander Shaw became the first African American chief justice, serving a two-year term.

In 2010, Republican gubernatorial candidate Rick Scott chose Jennifer Carroll as his running mate, and when she won, she became the first African American elected to statewide political office. Scott forced her out in 2013 amid an investigation into an illegal gambling ring, although she was never accused of wrongdoing.

37

MODERN FLORIDA

Florida's transition has been remarkable. On the eve of World War II, it was the least populated state in the South; at the turn of the twenty-first century, it was the fourth-largest state in the nation. In 2014, Florida passed New York to become the third-largest state in the United States.

In 1940, Florida was the twenty-seventh-largest state, sandwiched between South Carolina and Maryland and trailing Arkansas and West Virginia. When Florida became a state, one senator complained that it would never have the population of another state being admitted—Iowa. For a century, his prediction seemed to be true. It was not until the 1950 census that Florida passed Iowa.

The list of factors that changed the face of Florida is long. First came the automobile and the highways and then World War II brought hundreds of thousands of soldiers and sailors for training. Improvements in the speed and availability of airplanes, the Social Security Act, the ability to control insects and air conditioning also top the list.

In the twentieth century, Florida led the nation twice in population growth—51 percent in the 1920s and 78 percent in the 1950s. The 1970s saw a 43 percent rise. As historian Gary Mormino has pointed out, the population of the Disney theme parks on a single day is greater than the population of the entire state on the eve of the Civil War.

As late as 1900, Florida did not have any of the nation's one hundred largest cities. Florida finally made the list in 1910, when Jacksonville became the ninety-fifth-largest city, right behind Holyoke, Massachusetts, and three

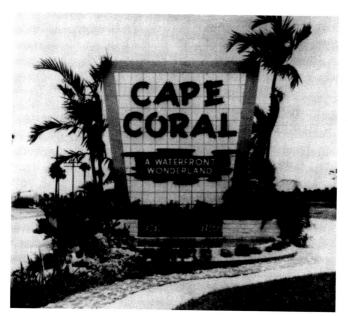

Cape Coral was an empty stretch of land in 1950, but within half a century, it had more than 150,000 residents, becoming the largest city in southwest Florida. Cape Coral was one of the communities that sold plots of land for a small down payment and monthly payments. *Florida Archives Photographic Collection.*

places behind East St. Louis, Illinois. Miami did not make the list until 1930, coming in at seventy-eighth place behind Wichita, Kansas.

And it has been a population on the move, constantly heading south. The original population stretched from Jacksonville to Pensacola. Towns like Live Oak were once in the list of the state's ten largest. As cotton and slavery vanished, the population moved toward South Florida.

American Express was the first company to establish a private pension plan starting in 1875. By 1929, there were nearly four hundred corporate pension plans, and the number was growing. By the 1950s, millions of Americans were covered by pensions and able to retire.

In 1940, Ida May Fuller of Vermont was issued the first Social Security check, receiving $22.54. It was enough to begin a population boom for Florida. When Ida May received her first check, there were 2,500 Social Security recipients in Florida, and by 2014, the number was closing in on four million.

The pensions and Social Security meant that retirees would have an income, even if small, and no longer had to depend on charity or family members. Homes in the North and Midwest turned into banks for the owners. A family buying a home in New Jersey at the end of World War II paid a median average price of $8,000. They could sell the house for $60,000 in 1980 and buy the same size house in Florida for half that much. A family could buy a home and add money to their retirement account.

TIMELINE 1969-2013

1969: Apollo 11 launches from Kennedy Space Center carrying the first men to land on the moon.

1971: Walt Disney World opens.

1980: Wave of Cuban immigrants in the Mariel boatlift brings 120,000 Cubans to Key West.

1980: Rehabilitation of South Beach hotels in Miami begins.

1981: The first space shuttle, *Columbia*, launches from Kennedy Space Center.

1990: Florida becomes the fourth-largest state as population surges.

1992: Hurricane Andrew hits South Florida.

2000: Presidential election between Al Gore and George W. Bush is decided in a controversial election in Florida.

2004–05: Wave of major hurricanes strike Florida.

2007: The Florida land boom collapses resulting in drastically reduced state revenue and falling home prices.

2010: With a population approaching nineteen million, Florida has the fourth-largest population and will pass New York for third place in 2014.

2010: End of the Space Shuttle Program at Kennedy Space Center in Cape Canaveral.

2012: Florida Southern College, which was designed by Frank Lloyd Wright, is designated as a National Historic Landmark.

2013: The 500th anniversary of Ponce de León's arrival in Florida.

Books with titles such as *How to Retire to Florida* in 1947 or *Florida Today: New Land of Opportunity* in 1950 became bestsellers. Unlike many popular books of the era, which supposedly told readers how to get rich, the message in these was that the average person could find a place to live in Florida or invest in land.

Developers quickly saw the possibilities. They introduced a new term—retirement community. In 1957, Leonard and Jack Rosen purchased a 103-square-mile tract near Fort Myers. It was so empty that local residents simply called it "the other side of the river." The two paid just $678,000 for the huge tract and called their two-man company Gulf American Corporation. They paved streets and began building houses. What the Rosens did best was sell lots. They dispatched salesmen throughout the North and West to convince people to buy the lots. No group was exempt from the sales pitch. Church dinners, Rotary Clubs and women's clubs all heard the pitch: put $20 down and pay $20 a month and when you are ready to retire, your beautiful home site on a canal will be waiting for you. Those who went to Cape Coral were flown over the area in one of five small planes to pick out their home site. When they found the one they wanted, the salesman dropped a bag of flour to mark the lot. Salesmen were dispatched overseas, where the lots proved popular, particularly in Germany. By 2010, the once empty land had 154,305 residents.

Between Orlando and Daytona Beach, the Mackle brothers purchased a vast track of empty land in 1962 and named it Deltona Lakes. They also began building, and by 2010, their development had become a city with a population of 85,182. The brothers also developed a large part of Key Biscayne and built what is now Palm Bay from empty brush and major developments in Port Charlotte and Port St. Lucie.

The ideas of the Rosens and the Mackles were repeated all over the state. Retirees flooded in, and soon it seemed appropriate that the state's official song was "The Old Folks at Home."

Besides Cape Coral and Deltona, one of the most successful retirement communities has been the Villages in Sumter County. In the 1960s, Harold Schwartz and Al Tarrson began selling land via mail order—a common sales tactic. When a federal law banned mail-order land sales, Schwartz and Tarrson tried a mobile home park. Schwartz bought out Tarrson and began to abandon the mobile home idea in favor of a community for retirees with lots of amenities. He brought in Gary Morse, whose vision created a vast community that has enough land to continue to grow for decades. By 2014, the population was approaching 100,000.

The average age of the population increased. In 1880, it was the nation's youngest state with a median age of eighteen. By 2014, Florida had one of the country's oldest populations.

The state and federal government both helped the development with road-building programs. In the 1950s, both began programs that remade Florida. The state built the Florida Turnpike in stages. The first section went from Fort Pierce to Miami along the coast. In 1964, the second section opened, linking Fort Pierce to Wildwood. In 1974 and 1986 more sections were added in South Florida.

In 1956, President Dwight Eisenhower began construction of the interstate highway system. One of the first was Interstate 4, which ran from Tampa to

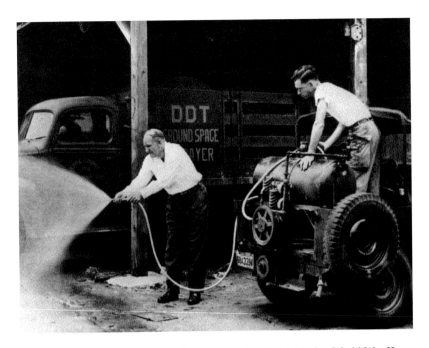

DDT was sprayed to control malaria and typhus in Florida during World War II and was seen as the answer to the problem of the mosquitoes that discouraged visitors and people moving to Florida. Shown to be harmful, it was banned for agricultural use in 1972. *Florida Archives Photographic Collection.*

Daytona Beach. The first section—from Plant City to Lakeland—opened in 1959, and the entire road was finished by the late 1960s.

Interstate 90 is the fourth-longest interstate highway, running from Jacksonville to Santa Monica, California. It runs the entire length of the Florida Panhandle. Interstate 95 runs from New England to Miami, and Interstate 275 goes down the west coast of Florida.

Not only would the highways bring in millions of tourists, but the interchanges would also attract malls, offices and homes.

Modern tourist attractions played a huge role in the economy of Florida. In 1933, during the Great Depression, 1 million tourists came to Florida. With the opening of Disney World, the number passed 10 million, and by 2014, it was approaching 100 million.

Florida's journey has been remarkable. In 1513, Ponce de León landed near Cape Canaveral. Over 450 years later, three men set off from the same spot for a journey to the moon. In between, residents have seen Florida go from cotton and slavery to oranges and vegetables to tourism and the space age.

And the journey is continuing.

FLORIDA'S COUNTIES AND ADMISSION DATES

Alachua (1824)
Baker (1861)
Bay (1913)
Bradford (1861)
Brevard (1855)
Broward (1915)
Calhoun (1838)
Charlotte (1921)
Citrus (1887)
Clay (1885)
Collier (1923)
Columbia (1832)
Dade (1836)
De Soto (1887)
Dixie (1921)
Duval (1822)
Escambia (1821)
Flagler (1917)
Franklin (1832)
Gadsden (1823
Gilchrist (1925)
Glades (1921)
Gulf (1925)

Hamilton (1827)
Hardee (1921)
Hendry (1923)
Hernando (1843)
Highlands (1921)
Hillsborough (1834)
Holmes (1848)
Indian River (1925)
Jackson (1822)
Jefferson (1827)
Lafayette (1856)
Lake (1887)
Lee (1887)
Leon (1824)
Levy (1845)
Liberty (1885)
Madison (1827)
Manatee (1855)
Marion (1844)
Martin (1925)
Monroe (1823)
Nassau (1824)
Okaloosa (1915)

Okeechobee (1917)
Orange (1845)
Osceola (1887)
Palm Beach (1909)
Pasco (1887)
Pinellas (1911)
Polk (1861)
Putnam (1849)
Santa Rosa (1842)
Sarasota (1921)
Seminole (1913)
St. Johns (1821)
St. Lucie (1844)
Sumter (1853)
Suwannee (1858)
Taylor (1856)
Union (1921)
Volusia (1854)
Wakulla (1843)
Walton (1824)
Washington (1829)

Appendix II

FLORIDA GOVERNORS

Governor	Term	Party
Andrew Jackson	1821	Territorial
William Pope Duval	1822–1834	Territorial
John Eaton	1834–1836	Territorial
Richard K. Call	1836–1839	Territorial
Robert R. Reid	1839–1841	Territorial
Richard K. Call	1841–1844	Territorial
John Branch	1844–1845	Territorial
William Moseley	1845–1849	Democratic
Thomas Brown	1849–1853	Whig
James E. Broome	1853–1857	Democratic
Madison S. Perry	1857–1861	Democratic
John Milton	1861–1865	Democratic
Abraham K. Allison	1865	Democratic
William Marvin	1865	Provisional
Davis S. Walker	1865–1868	Democratic
Harrison Reed	1868–1873	Republican
Ossian B. Hart	1873–1874	Republican

GOVERNOR	TERM	PARTY
Marcellus Stearns	1874–1877	Republican
George F. Drew	1877–1881	Democratic
William Bloxham	1881–1885	Democratic
Edward A. Perry	1885–1889	Democratic
Francis P. Fleming	1889–1893	Democratic
Henry L. Mitchell	1893–1897	Democratic
William D. Bloxham	1897–1901	Democratic
William S. Jennings	1901–1905	Democratic
Napoleon Broward	1905–1909	Democratic
Albert W. Gilchrist	1909–1913	Democratic
Park Trammell	1913–1917	Democratic
Sidney J. Catts	1917–1921	Prohibition
Gary A. Hardee	1921–1925	Democratic
John W. Martin	1925–1929	Democratic
Doyle E. Carlton	1929–1933	Democratic
David Sholtz	1933–1937	Democratic
Fred P. Cone	1937–1941	Democratic
Spessard Holland	1941–1945	Democratic
Millard F. Caldwell	1945–1949	Democratic
Fuller Warren	1949–1953	Democratic
Daniel McCarty	1953	Democratic
Charley Johns	1953–1955	Democratic
Leroy Collins	1955–1961	Democratic
Farris Bryant	1961–1965	Democratic
Haydon Burns	1965–1967	Democratic
Claude Kirk	1967–1971	Republican
Reubin Askew	1971–1979	Democratic
Bob Graham	1979–1987	Democratic

GOVERNOR	TERM	PARTY
Wayne Mixson	1987	Democratic
Bob Martinez	1987–1991	Republican
Lawton Chiles	1991–1998	Democratic
Buddy McKay	1998–1999	Democratic
Jeb Bush	1999–2007	Republican
Charlie Crist	2007–2011	Republican
Rick Scott	2011–present	Republican

BIBLIOGRAPHY

Akerman, Joe A. *Florida Cowman: A History of Florida Cattle Raising.* Kissimmee: Florida Cattlemen's Association, 1976.

Akin, Edward N. *Flagler, Rockefeller Partner and Florida Baron.* Kent, OH: Kent State University Press, 1988.

Arsenault, Raymond. "The End of the Long Hot Summer: The Air Conditioner and Southern Culture." *Journal of Southern History* 50, no. 4 (1984): 597–628.

Barnes, Jay. *Florida's Hurricane History.* Chapel Hill: University of North Carolina Press, 1998.

Bolton, Herbert Eugene. *The Spanish Borderlands: A Chronicle of Old Florida and the Southwest.* New Haven, CT: Yale University Press, 1921.

Clark, James C. *Pineapple Anthology of Florida Writers.* Vol. 1. Sarasota, FL: Pineapple Press, 2013.

———. *Presidents in Florida: How the Presidents Have Shaped Florida and How Florida Has Influenced the Presidents.* Sarasota, FL: Pineapple Press, 2012.

Coker, William S., and Jerrell H. Shofner. *Florida: From the Beginning to 1992; A Columbus Jubilee Commemorative.* Houston, TX: Pioneer Publications, 1991.

Colburn, David R. *The African American Heritage of Florida.* Gainesville: University Press of Florida, 1995 .

———. *From Yellow Dog Democrats to Red State Republicans: Florida and Its Politics Since 1940.* Gainesville: University Press of Florida, 2007.

Colburn, David R., and Richard K. Scher. *Florida's Gubernatorial Politics in the Twentieth Century.* Gainesville: University Presses of Florida, 1980.

Covington, James W. *The Seminoles of Florida*. Gainesville: University Press of Florida, 1993.

Davis, Jack E., and Raymond Arsenault., eds. *Paradise Lost: The Environmental History of Florida*. Gainesville: University Press of Florida, 2005.

Derr, Mark. *Some Kind of Paradise: A Chronicle of Man and the Land in Florida*. New York: W. Morrow, 1989.

Gannon, Michael. *The New History of Florida*. Gainesville: University Press of Florida, 1996.

————. *Operation Drumbeat: The Dramatic True Story of Germany's First U-boat Attacks Along the American Coast in World War II*. New York: Harper & Row, 1990.

George, Paul S. *A Guide to the History of Florida*. New York: Greenwood Press, 1989.

Johns, John Edwin. *Florida During the Civil War*. Gainesville: University of Florida Press, 1963.

Lyon, Eugene. *Pedro Menendez de Aviles*. New York: Garland Pub., 1995.

Milanich, Jerald T. *Florida's Indians from Ancient Times to the Present*. Gainesville: University Press of Florida, 1998.

Milanich, Jerald T., and Susan Milbrath. *First Encounters: Spanish Explorations in the Caribbean and the United States, 1492–1570*. Gainesville: University of Florida Press, 1989.

Miller, Randall M. *Shades of the Sunbelt Essays on Ethnicity, Race, and the Urban South*. New York: Greenwood Press, 1988.

Mormino, Gary Ross. *Land of Sunshine, State of Dreams: a Social History of Modern Florida*. Gainesville: University Press of Florida, 2005.

Mormino, Gary Ross, and George E. Pozzetta. *The Immigrant World of Ybor City Italians and Their Latin Neighbors in Tampa, 1885–1985*. Gainesville: University Press of Florida, 1998.

Noll, Steven, and David Tegeder. *Ditch of Dreams: The Cross Florida Barge Canal and the Struggle for Florida's Future*. Gainesville: University Press of Florida, 2009.

Patrick, Rembert W., and Allen Covington Morris. *Florida Under Five Flags*. 4th ed. Gainesville: University of Florida Press, 1967.

Revels, Tracy J. *Grander in Her Daughters: Florida's Women During the Civil War*. Columbia: University of South Carolina Press, 2004.

————. *Sunshine Paradise: A History of Florida Tourism*. Gainesville: University Press of Florida, 2011.

Rothchild, John. *Up for Grabs: A Trip Through Time and Space in the Sunshine State*. New York: Viking, 1985.

Shofner, Jerrell H. *Nor Is It Over Yet: Florida in the Era of Reconstruction, 1863–1877*. Gainesville: University Presses of Florida, 1974.

Tebeau, Charlton W. *A History of Florida*. Coral Gables, FL: University of Miami Press, 1971.

Tebeau, Charlton W., and William Marina. *A History of Florida*. 3rd ed. Coral Gables, FL: University of Miami Press, 1999.

Virga, Vincent, and E. Lynne Wright. *Florida, Mapping the Sunshine State Through History Rare and Unusual Maps from the Library of Congress*. Guilford, CT: Globe Pequot Press, 2011.

Wright, J. Leitch. *Florida in the American Revolution*. Gainesville: University Presses of Florida, 1975.

INDEX